From the genocide that left Rwanda reeling,
to a new vision for a brighter future, *The Noble Dream!*
is a remarkable story you won't soon forget.

Charles Mugisha Buregeya,
founder of Africa New Life Ministries International,
shares his journey from unimaginable suffering
to hope in an unchanging God.

Read this book. Share it with others. And join Charles
in sharing the Love capable of mending
the brokenhearted and catalyzing radical reconciliation.

**—Kevin Palau, President,
Palau Association**

The Noble Dream!

From the Jungles of Uganda
To the Hills of Rwanda
Faith Prevails

Charles Mugisha Buregeya
with Susan W. Lester

The Noble Dream!
From the Jungles of Uganda
To the Hills of Rwanda
Faith Prevails

*Special thanks to Susan W. Lester, without whom this book
never would have been written. Additional thanks to David
Sanford, who served as the book's editor and recommended
the two-track auto\biographical format.*

Part of the proceeds from the sale of this book will go to
help support the multi-faceted ministries of the author
and Africa New Life Ministries International.

Published by
Africa New Life Ministries International
7145 SW Varns St., Suite 201, Portland, OR 97223
africanewlife.org
book@africanewlife.org
(503) 906-1590

Available for sale from the publisher
and many online retailers including
- www.CreateSpace.com
- www.Borders.com
- www.BooksaMillion.com
- www.BarnesandNoble.com
- www.Amazon.com

To all family members
and our many friends,
wonderful mentors,
ministry partners,
board of directors,
staff members,
prayer partners,
child sponsors,
and other donors
and supporters
who
by God's leading, blessing,
wisdom and generosity have made
Africa New Life Ministries International
what it is today...

thank you!

Shaking a Nation

*For we must come to see that peace is not merely the absence of
some negative force, it is the presence of a positive force. True
peace is not merely the absence of tension, but it is the presence
of justice and brotherhood.*
—*Martin Luther King*

*This is my commandment, that you love one another,
even as I have loved you.*
—*Jesus Christ*

When you pick coffee, you must use two hands. What one
hand cannot reach, the other hand can reach. That is why
Africa New Life Ministries focuses on two things—acts of
compassion and the proclamation of God's Word. If you have
only one hand, you are crippled, you cannot be effective. So
we have two hands, joined in one goal—to bring hope and new
life to the poor, the orphans, the widows, all of the hurting
people of Rwanda.

Charles Mugisha Buregeya often speaks of his ministry with
these words, keeping these principles in the foreground.

No one knows better than Charles Buregeya that Rwandans
are a hurting people. He and his wife, Florence, have committed
their lives to them.

Over the past forty-five years, throughout the Tutsi
persecutions by the Hutus which culminated in the genocide of
1994 when more than 800,000 men, women and children were
slaughtered, and even now as the nation of Rwanda slowly
rebuilds, Rwandans have suffered terribly.

Because of the mass killings their family structure has been
destroyed; their properties lay fallow or vandalized or simply
abandoned; their personal remembrances are of horror—many

times too painful to be embraced—resulting in depression, post traumatic symptoms or even mental illness. Their lives are threatened with HIV, poverty, and hopelessness.

And, beneath the surface, there is deep emotional trauma and spiritual struggle as recently released prisoners, who were responsible for the murder of their neighbors, must once again live in communities with the genocide survivors.

Against the backdrop of this darkness shines the life of Charles Mugisha Buregeya and the ministry of Africa New Life Ministries International.

Founded by Charles and his wife, Florence, Africa New Life Ministries is not just one man's philanthropic effort, attempting to put band-aids over a nightmare of suffering.

Instead, it is a beacon of hope for lasting impact and community transformation. It is the embodiment of what God's Son, Jesus Christ, meant when he commanded us to "love one another."

The passion for Africa New Life Ministries (ANLM) comes not from platitudes, a desire to do good deeds, or political objectives. It comes from God. So, we trust as you read this book that the Lord's compassion, His dream-giving, and His love for the Rwandan people clearly shine as beacons of hope.

Driving along in the car on the way to the ANLM Portland office, Alan Hotchkiss, Africa New Life's Executive Director, turns to Charles and says, "Hey, I just read Psalm 20 this morning and it was really good stuff."

Charles flips to it and reads it aloud:

> *"May the Lord answer you in the day of trouble! May the name of the God of Jacob set you securely on high! May He send you help from the sanctuary, and support you from Zion! May He remember all your meal offerings, and find your burnt offering acceptable! Selah."*
>
> *"May He grant you your heart's desire, and fulfill all your counsel! We will sing for joy over your victory. And in the name of our God we will set up our banners. May the Lord fulfill all your petitions."*
>
> *"Now I know that the Lord saves His anointed; He will answer him from His holy heaven, with the saving strength of*

His right hand. Some boast in chariots, and some in horses; but we will boast in the name of the Lord, our God. They have bowed down and fallen; but we have risen and stood upright. Save O Lord; may the King answer us in the day we call."

You know, Alan, this Scripture passage reminds me of a story about a tiny ant who climbed onto an elephant and was clinging to his back. The elephant crossed a bridge and the bridge was shaking, shaking in a big way. So the ant says to himself, "Wow, look at me! I am shaking a bridge!" But it was really the elephant doing the shaking.

We are like that little ant. We are on God's back (not that God is as small as an elephant—you know He's much bigger!) and we are clinging to Him. It is God that does the shaking. We don't really do the shaking. So God is the winner. He is the winner! We need to give Him the praise and the glory for the shaking!

What can change hatred into love? What power can transform a nation that lost more than 10 percent of its population in a genocidal blood bath?

What can mend the broken hearts and spirits of those transformed by anger, used by politicians, forsaken by church leaders, and overwhelmed by prejudices and fear?

How can this small nation be reunited—murderers with victims—now again living side by side?

It is the same power that kept a family alive through two wars in two nations. It is the same power that stirred the inner heart of a child soldier in Uganda to receive the Gospel. It is the same power that brought that boy into manhood and carried him across continents to share the freedom he had found in Christ. And it is that power that called this man, Charles Mugisha Buregeya, a man of faith, to help the hurting in Rwanda.

As you will discover as you read his story, Charles is riding on the back of that force—the gracious, love-giving, new-life-giving power of God Almighty, maker of heaven and earth.

And God is doing the shaking!

Chapter 1

In the Triangle

*Every gun that is made, every warship launched, every rocket
fired signifies in the final sense, a theft from those who hunger
and are not fed, those who are cold and are not clothed.
This world in arms is not spending money alone.
It is spending the sweat of its laborers, the genius of its
scientists, and the hopes of its children.
This is not a way of life at all in any true sense.
Under the clouds of war, it is humanity
hanging on a cross of iron.*
*—President Dwight D. Eisenhower, speech,
American Society of Newspaper Editors, 16 April 1953*

I was walking home in the dark from a nearby village, scanning
the path for snakes. Since the bush was thick and the path
was small, it was very dark. The moon was waning and the
trees were rattling in a slight wind, clapping their branches
together. *The spirits must not be happy tonight,* I thought.

At thirteen and the oldest, my parents often sent me to the
market to get small things like salt or sugar or coffee.

This time by the time I had found the needed item and
paid for it, darkness was already falling, and soon the only light
would be from the moon as it rose over the close rows of
banana trees.

Then I saw someone in the middle of the path ahead. *Was
it a man with a machete?* I wondered. *He might be waiting for
me.* My skin began to prickle as I clenched the tobacco my
father was waiting to have before bed. I stopped, calculating
my options, staring harder at the image ahead. If I turned and
ran away quickly, I might be able to escape; if I am caught I

might take a beating, or worse... *Maybe that isn't a machete*, I thought hopefully.

My heart was pounding but I knew I had to get home. I must finish my job. Squaring my shoulders I decided to face my fear and charged straight down the path, my head down. I ran, veering as far to the opposite side of the path as I possibly could, telling my feet to fly swifter than they ever had before.

As I neared the man melted into a shadow; the moonlight behind a banana tree stump had caused the illusion.

Many of the things we fear in our lives are not real. The devil specializes in putting shadows in front of you, especially when there is something you are supposed to do for God. So you must face your fears—they are not real if they exist only in your minds.

The circumference of your own mind is so small; it is a complete lie to trust in your own little brain. Only Jesus knows if you will have both of your legs tomorrow, or both of your ears, or whether you will eat. Have the reality of the person of Jesus Christ in your life every day. He is omniscient so why don't you trust in Him?

As he finishes telling this story to a room full of church members, Charles opens his hands to the sky and laughs. But, the reality of men with machetes was not an idle fear for Charles as a child. He lived with his parents in Uganda where they had fled after both of their families had been murdered in Rwanda by machete-toting killers.

The history of the ethnic conflict in Rwanda began with Colonial rule. The Belgians elevated the Tutsis, one of three tribal groups, educating them and offering them training to oversee their plantations. They also instigated a system to record the ethnicity of each student attending school. This began a class distinction and smoldering resentments among the more populous Hutu. When the Tutsis decided they wanted independence in 1959, the Belgians encouraged a bloody Hutu revolt resulting in a wave of massacres of the Tutsi elite.

By the time Belgium pulled out of Rwanda in 1962, a Hutu government based on the so-called "Hutu revolution" headed by Gregory Kayibanda was firmly in place. Later in a political coup in 1973, Major General Jenvinal Habyarimana took over power but did nothing to unite the Rwandans.

By this time Tutsis had become second-class citizens, often facing persecution, violence, and death at the hands of Hutu extremists. Tens of thousands died over these decades due to a series of massacres of Tutsis by Hutus, winked at or encouraged by the government.[1] Many others fled the country, with thousands pouring across the borders into Tanzania and Uganda.

Following the death of their families in one of the early slaughters in the 1960s, Konsalata Mukamusoni, Charles's mother, and Aloyizi Buregeya, his father, both fled to the Masaka area in Uganda.

Masaka is a city located 80 miles southwest of Kampala on Lake Victoria and is very close to the equator. Most of the people in Masaka are farmers with cattle and crops. At that time it was also the highest producer of the indigenous banana food locally referred to as *Matooke*. It was a good area for a new beginning and many Rwandan refugees settled there.

Charles's parents fell in love and got married, but at that time going back to Rwanda was not an option. Persecutions against anyone Tutsi were growing. Often reports came of more brutal attacks, local family groups wiped out by government soldiers in trumped up raids.

In Uganda they were able to find good work, build a home, raise cattle, develop a coffee plantation of their own, and send their children to school.

Charles, born in Uganda, already had visited that dark cool space where self remains when injury and prejudice mount their brutal onslaughts. Bullies abounded for a kid whose parents were refugees from Rwanda, and worse than the physical threats made good in bloody noses were the bruises others could not see. Those deep wounds were gouged out from weary days of a life being told over and over again that he was nothing: not needed, not worthy, not accepted, not valuable.

"Life was very hard," says Charles simply, and for a short moment he revisits that battered place, his eyes closing, exhaling slowly. "But God got us through that!" he states with firm resolution.

Peace in Uganda would not last long. Idi Amin Dada was not a good leader. Uganda was in increasing disarray; his reign became erratic, filled with atrocities levied against anyone who opposed him or whom he simply disliked.

As a Muslim, Idi Amin made a practice of persecuting Christians along with his enemies. Many of his policies promoted Muslim superiority and prosperity. The Catholic priests had been threatened not to spread their religion by Idi Amin's soldiers, and some of the priests were beaten. But the Catholic Church was very powerful. Too many Ugandans went to Catholic churches, and nuns and priests taught the children in schools they built and staffed. Idi Amin couldn't risk negative international attention by becoming too aggressive with them.

Evangelicals, however, were prime targets along with anyone suspected of siding with Idi Amin's enemies. Around this time, Charles saw a woman evangelist on the street proclaiming Jesus Christ, telling others around her to "get saved" before it was too late. No one paid much mind to her because she was a woman, uneducated, and fearlessly shouting her messages along the roadside. *She's a crazy one,* Charles thought, but he also wondered at her fearlessness. What was her motivation to risk death?

Idi Amin's reign of terror came abruptly to an end when his war with Tanzania failed, in part due to insurrections against him in his own country. He was chased from the country. By this time, many in his army had already deserted him, some with political agendas of their own. This brought on a time of intense competition and fighting for governmental power.

The culmination of these struggles came when general elections in 1980 were "won" by Milton Obote's Uganda People's Congress. Yoweri Museveni, then the leader of the rival Uganda Patriotic Movement party, alleged electoral fraud and declared an armed rebellion, plunging the country into civil war.

As Uganda fell into the Luweero War, so named for the region where most of the fighting occurred, Charles's father, Aloyizi Buregeya, developed his own plans. He would not see his family slaughtered as his parents were in Rwanda. Instead, war called for survival strategy. Aloyizi began to contact all of his relatives, especially those in safer areas.

8

In Rwanda, family is very important. It is an obligation to help one's family members any time there is a need if you have the means. You do it because you know these same family members will help you when you need it one day. You do it because it is socially expected. Aloyizi knew his family would help him with his plan.

"Come with me," Aloyizi said one day, in a serious tone. Obediently, Charles followed him out through the little mounds where they grew their sweet potatoes. Charles was barely fourteen years old, but had grown in stature. He no longer feared men in the shadows. Instead, he had the confidence of a youthful lion.

Aloyizi was carrying a small tin box. In it was a considerable amount of cash. They buried it and planted a yam plant on top of it. As he brushed dry dirt from his hands, Aloyizi said to his eldest son, "If war comes, and we don't make it, you will know where to dig." Not long after that, his mother buried their fine China, the beautiful porcelain plates and cups they used for guests. Most families were not that well off and she knew they would be stolen from their home.

The Luweero District became the site of a fierce insurgency by the rebel group National Resistance Army (NRA) under the leadership of Museveni and of a brutal counter-insurgency by the government of Milton Obote. It was a large area, dense with bush, where the guerrilla forces could easily hide and regroup. And it was full of sympathetic villagers.

Obote's soldiers began to raid villages in the area, rounding up more of the citizens, dragging them off or beating them. Obote had made it clear to his troops that the Rwandans were to be treated as the enemy, forcing them to join the guerrillas. Many thousands of civilians died during the early to mid 1980s in this civil war, and a large number of them were Rwandan refugees.

Charles remembers the struggles the families in his village went though trying to decide how to protect their children and where they should go. Some of his family's close friends decided to cross over to the areas controlled by Museveni, and Aloyizi decided that Charles would be safer there, too.

I left my father and mother and went with our family friends to the Nakaseke area. It was there that I became involved in the war—really because I had no choice. It was expected that everyone in the area would help with security for the guerrillas. There was no middle ground. If you didn't help the resistance, you would be considered an enemy of the liberation. Everyone knew who you were and since Obote was killing Rwandans, it was only right, according to the men in charge, that everyone fight for the freedom to live. I was young, only fourteen. We were told it was the thing we must do—fight for liberation. Looking back, I think it was a kind of brain-washing.

I was a child being used by men who wanted to get power and take over the government. Children are the most vulnerable people of a community. But now, I hate war. I don't ever want to be involved in another war. Children should not have to be involved in these things. They are innocent. They must be protected within a society.

As he speaks of his time in the bush with the guerrilla forces, Charles hesitates often, his brow wrinkles, his shoulders appear to be pressed down by some unseen hands. The memories are difficult to bear, even now. He reveals only bits and pieces, reluctant to recount the brutalities and atrocities of guerrilla warfare.

As the war escalated rapidly, Charles's father put the rest of his plan into motion. There was no other choice. The refugees in the camp where they were staying had told them to go and hide in the swamp. They said, "When the attackers come you will put all of the rest of us in danger. You cannot keep young children quiet while you hide. You cannot control them." But there were Tsetse flies and mosquitoes in the swamp. If they hid there, the children would probably die from sleeping sickness or malaria. They had to move on. So, Konsalata and her children were sent by bus, an ancient vehicle with holes everywhere, to stay with Aloyizi's brother in a small village near Masaka. Joseph was nine; Fred and Specioza were still toddlers.

The house was rough, dirt floors, thatched roofing made from banana leaves and wooden branches. The sides were full of holes. They slept on the floor, the goats in the hut with them. There was the unending drone of flies, gnats, and other crawling bugs joining them in the hut. The next day they ate with their hands off the same plate. It wasn't a plate really; it was a platter. There were no utensils. Joseph couldn't eat.

They went to the bus station to say goodbye to their mother. Joseph stood quietly by while the other two children cried and carried on. His mother thought this was odd because the day before he had begged her constantly to take him away with her. She was right—nine-year-old Joseph had a plan. Just before the bus began to move, Joseph broke into a run and jumped aboard, the door closing abruptly behind him.

"Stop! Stop the bus! He can't come! He must get off!" Konsalata yelled at the driver. Others on the bus tried to get the driver to stop but he just shook his head and the rickety bus rattled away. He wasn't in the mood to deal with a family scene or to delay the bus schedule. Joseph slept all the way home on his mother's lap.

Meanwhile, Charles was in the middle of the area where the fiercest fighting occurred. It was a war of cat and mouse. They assigned him to a post as a child intelligence officer. As such, Charles would infiltrate the small communities, selling sugar and salt at the markets. He got to know who came in and who went out, found out many things by just hanging around, turning in the information he found out would sometimes lead to the death of government forces.

This was a war where children were often used as bait, Charles included. The guerillas would assign a younger child to stand at a makeshift road block. Charles almost always had this as a nightly assignment.

> I had a machete and a spear. Several other children hid nearby in the bushes. When a person approached, if he put his hands up, as if he was surrendering, he was okay. Everyone knew this was how to approach a roadblock. He would then present a paper on which orders were written for those out at night wishing passage. If he had no paper or approached with attitude or questioned the roadblock, he would be ambushed,

because he did not respect the authority of the guerillas behind the roadblock. We assumed he was an enemy.

When government troops were spotted in the area, a runner would be sent to warn us or we would hear the drums. Then we would run into the bush, splitting up and working our way back to the main troop commanders. Commanders decided who did what. It was a dangerous, exhausting duty, as government soldiers traveled the roads often looking for the guerrillas.

I prayed every night for protection. I had been taught in the Catholic schools and at church that God would protect you when you prayed. I remember walking with the others along narrow dark paths, snaking our way through the bush of the Luweero Triangle toward new areas of safety or confrontation, and how I prayed for protection. Land mines could potentially take off my legs. The government soldiers could be right around the next tree, ready to open fire.

The nights were long and dark; there were no lights and the moon was often blocked by the bush. We kept going because our commanders told us we were fighting for a freer Uganda. Sometimes we would drink banana beer to help with the fear.

In the Luweero War, or "The War in the Bush," staying alive as a child soldier meant doing whatever you were told. If you didn't obey orders you were beaten or killed. Often, child soldiers were sent ahead of the militia as decoys, told to engage the enemy, flushing out the government forces. Some had guns, many did not. Then the militia would flank the government troops.

During this conflict, from 1981 to 1985, thousands of Ugandan children from ten to eighteen years old were taken from their villages, many in brutal raids where some saw their parents murdered and their homes looted. They were forced to serve on one side or the other of conflicts they didn't understand. Most of them died.

Sadly, thousands more children have been involuntarily forced into soldiering since the Luweero War, as the Lord's Resistance Army has continued to rebel against the government, using village raids to steal children, often murdering their parents. Recently the Congress of the United States of America has passed and President Obama has signed a bill to help Uganda defeat and disarm the LRA once and for all, with the hopes of bringing peace again to Uganda, especially to the children.[2]

For two long years, Charles ran, hid, spied, guarded the roads, fought and suffered the loss of friends, youth, and innocence.

Although the family he was living with was very kind to him, Charles missed his parents and his brothers and sisters. Often, in the darkness of a lonely night, he would feel the weight of it in his chest, as if his heart was reaching out for them across the dark forests. Then a rumor surfaced that Aloyizi was dead. Not long after that someone else said that they had seen Charles's father in a market.

>*Was my father dead or alive? What was happening to my mother?* These thoughts plagued my mind constantly. No one could tell me for sure. I had to know; I couldn't stand it any longer. I began to plot my escape.
>
>I had to hide it from my family friends. They had promised my father they would keep me safe so they would not have let me go. They knew I might be killed along the way or if the NRA officers found out, they would order a search. Deserters could be ambushed, captured, and then give away information in the process of torture so they were usually tracked down and shot.
>
>Also, apart from that, it was very complicated to cross from the area where we were to the area where my parents were last spotted. The one long road that divided the two areas was constantly patrolled by military with mortars and tanks. Land mines covered some of the few passages between the two areas.
>
>So, I began to make friends with men in a more dangerous guerilla group who already had permission to go farther into the danger zones. In the process I told them about my deep desire to find my father, to see if he was alive or not, just to verify it. Many of the soldiers were sympathetic to my love for my father and concern for my family, so they agreed to help me. They convinced the military officials that I was willing

to spy in more dangerous areas and so I was allowed to go with them.

Finally, the night came; I was going back! It was a long night, creeping through the bush. We didn't dare use our machetes. We moved as quietly as we could, hoping not to attract enemy attention. We also watched for leopards and snakes, always a present danger. I began to pray. As the night grew darker, I could see less and less.

As far back as I could remember my family had gone to the Catholic Church. I had come into the world two months early, the result of my mother's stress from the death of my brother. My parents had brought my brother to the hospital with a case of the measles but it was too late. My parents found a priest and had me baptized, thinking I might not survive, believing that death would mean eternal hell if I wasn't sprinkled with holy water first.

In the second grade I memorized the Catholic catechism and taught it to my friends in school. I had a prayer book and was taught to pray to the saints and to Mother Mary for protection. I was told they would take my prayers to God. Father Joseph, a Catholic priest in Uganda, taught me that God was listening. I believed that God loved me and that was why I was still alive. God would bring me through this night too.

Suddenly there was a sound in the bush, something was moving toward us. In a panic, to get away from the sound, I ran straight for one of the men who happened to be carrying a grenade. The sudden movement and sound startled him. Normally, the soldier with the grenade would open the pin and throw it toward the bush, hoping to stop an ambush before it happened. Fortunately he had not pulled the pin from his grenade and didn't throw it. Otherwise, it would have hit me and most surely I would be dead.

The night wore on without any other incidents. The soldiers took me across the path of land mines, showing me where to step and where not to step. As dawn began to break, the soldiers left me to go my own way. They had brought me near to a small military post, the area where my father was supposed to have been seen. Fortunately, I met a guerrilla military official who used to be my friend. He was concerned for the family he had left in the area where I had just come from and wanted to know about them, so he never thought to ask for any paperwork.

During this time, the guerillas were fast losing ground and the fighting in the area where Charles had been had became vicious and relentless. Looking back, Charles believes that God guided him, even before he really knew it. Many of the soldiers and villagers in that area died over the next days from raids by the government troops.

A few days later, thanks to the Lord's sovereignty and providence, Charles was delighted to find his mother and father, and Emma, Joseph and Rose. It was unbelievable; what a happy reunion! Their troubles, however, were far from over.

Now the whole family was on the run constantly, running away from antitank bombs and mortar shells lobbed into villages where the government forces thought guerillas were hiding. Many of the homes were already burned to the ground, and the family spent many sleepless nights in the bush watching and waiting and hiding or seeking safer shelter.

One day Charles and Emma went to get water from a well. The whole family had been going without water for some time since soldiers in the area were watching most of the water sources. The family couldn't go on any longer. At the well, Charles loaded water on the back of the bicycle they used and Emma put a large jug on his head. Just after getting the water, they heard the military guns fire and bullets poured down around them like rain.

Abandoning the water they ran through the woods. A piece of wood ripped through Charles leg as mortar fire blasted it from a nearby tree.

The family managed to get some medicine for Charles's leg, but it wasn't enough to take a prescribed treatment orally. So, Charles decided that maybe the medicine would work if he poured it directly on the wound.

Everyone knew that the capsules were good medicine but, since there were no doctors, they didn't know they were meant to be swallowed. As a result, the wound did not heal and began to fester. Would his leg be permanently ruined?

Chapter 2

Betrayals and Escapes

Blessed be the Lord, who daily bears our burden, the God who is our salvation. Selah. God is to us a God of deliverances; and to God the Lord belong escapes from death.
—Psalms 68:19-20

*A man's steps are directed by the Lord,
How then can anyone understand his own way?*
—Proverbs 21:24

A group of families, including the Buregeyas, decided to surrender to the government military. For two years they had been suffering, often going without food, and many had painful injuries or were sick. Charles himself was very sick from the wound in his leg, now a black, rancid mess that he could no longer cover with his hand.

They all were put into an internment camp, which was really a village called Kicyusa (pronounced *Ca-chu-sa*).

All of the political prisoners were taken to Kicyusa, as well, so all of the roads in and out were blocked and patrolled. Families were forced to live in large groups to make it easier to monitor them. The soldiers would roam through the village and kill anybody from the camp if they had any reason to think they were still connected to the guerilla groups.

The soldiers would also take and rape the women. If a man stood up to the soldiers raping his wife, he was killed. A soldier would come and take a woman from her father, her mother, or her husband and make her stay in his tent. She would serve as his wife. It was agony for the family, for her husband, seeing her every day with someone else, against her will, but what could they do? They had no weapons and there was no one to tell.

There was no privacy and no food, so the villagers snuck out to go to gardens around the camp to steal food. Sometimes NGO organizations brought in some food. Villagers were also forced to go outside the camps for water. Thankfully, Charles received medical treatment for his wound from the Red Cross, which saved his leg and probably his life; many other wounds were treated and healed as well.

One night the soldiers came and took a group of men, including Charles and Aloyizi, out of the village to guard their stolen cows. Early the next morning they were told to take the cows to a village a full days' walk away. This had never happened before and the men wondered among themselves what was going on, but of course they didn't ask questions.

Konsalata woke with a start, thinking maybe Charles and Aloyizi were returning. She crawled to the entrance of their small shack. It was very quiet. *Where were the government soldiers who usually guarded the enclosure?* she wondered to herself. And then she heard it—the unmistakable death scream of one of her neighbors. She grabbed the baby, Godfrey, and his brother Emanuel (Emma for short.)

"Wake up, Joseph, take Rose and run! Don't stop until you get into the bush!" she said as quietly as she could while she shook him awake.

He leapt up immediately, grabbed Rose out of her bed, and began to run to the back of the compound. Konsalata ran in the other direction. Rebel soldiers were blocking her way so she hid herself with her two children as best as she could. Then the screaming began in earnest.

Why were the rebel soldiers here? Why were they killing everyone? Tears of fear and horror ran freely down her cheeks. Suddenly, Konsalata could feel herself being tugged backward. The rebel soldiers had found her hiding spot. They pushed her quickly forward; most of them had machetes, dripping with blood. As day broke they took her with them as they left, along with many others. She wondered why they didn't kill her. Maybe they were just tired of killing. But there were worse things than killing.

Further from the compound now and deeper into the jungle, the rebel soldiers paused to catch their breath. They took her to the leader. She was still holding both of her children tightly, afraid to let go. *They are going to kill us,* she thought, *so why don't they get it over with?*

The leader spoke to the others, "I know her," and then asked, "Konsalata, where is your son, Charles? He is a good militia but we haven't seen him in some time."

She turned her head down, looking at her children's heads, hoping to say the right thing. She knew they would kill her or perhaps use her as a "wife." A tear crept down her cheek. Her voice weak with sorrow and fear, she said, "He is dead; the government soldiers killed him." It was a lie. She hoped they couldn't tell.

The leader looked at her carefully, then he motioned his hand as if she were a fly to be brushed off, and they left her alone. A friend of Charles, one of the rebels, recognized her and took her with him. He had family members on the other side of the war, fighting among the rebels. He decided to use Konsalata to carry a message to his relatives—to warn them not to cross over but to stay where they were. The rebels were losing and the fighting was worse than ever. In return he protected her from the other soldiers and did not harm her or her children. After a few weeks he helped her escape and escorted her some distance so that she could carry the message to his family members.

Meanwhile, the men had delivered the cattle to the village. They were paid with a beating; Charles was able to run away but Aloyizi and some of the other men were struck down, beaten, and then left to fend for themselves. As soon as they could, they left quickly, hurrying back to their families, only to hear on the way reports of the slaughter at the internment camp. Knowing the compound was about to be attacked by the rebel soldiers, the government soldiers had their stolen cattle removed. In their minds that had been the only thing worth saving.

It took two days but during the journey different government soldiers were sent to escort them safely back to the camp. Most likely the Red Cross had been protesting their treatment. On the final day, a huge lorry loaded with goods came along. The men hopped on and rode through the night, wondering what they would find when they arrived. Charles recounts the scene as if it were yesterday; the stress of it shows again on his face, his breath shortens.

As the sun began to rise, I entered the camp with the other men. There were dead bodies everywhere. Since the village was large, many people had escaped into the bush to hide but 150 others lay around us, their bodies twisted in death and beginning to swell in the relentless sun. Most had been murdered with machetes, and a few had been shot.

Running into our assigned space in the compound, my father heaved a heavy sigh—my mother and the other four children were not there. Still panic stricken, my father yelled to me, "Go and look for them! Go and look for them!"

We ran frantically through the compound and searched through the corpses. Finally we stopped and just stood there in the silence. We were numb with despair. None of our five precious ones were among the dead, but many of our friends and neighbors were.

I stood in that village among the dead as darkness covered me. A coldness entered my bones, an unwelcome feeling crouched in the corner of my mind, taunting me with an unanswerable question: *Why aren't you dead too?*

We moved into the center of the camp for more security and protection. The rebels had taken everything from our home—all of our clothes, cooking utensils, food, even our clothing—there was nothing left but one of my sweaters with one sleeve missing.

It was late evening when a movement caught our eye. "Papa, we are here!" said Joseph. He had Rose by one hand and a rope tied to one of our cows in the other. Joseph told us he had hidden with her in the bush and when they heard the engine of the lorry bringing the men back, they followed the sound.

It was a joyful reunion and then my father said, "What of your mother and our babies?"

"I don't know," Joseph said. "I don't know!"

The war had stripped away most of what Aloyizi had, except for his love for his native country. He felt a startling sense of hopelessness; always before he could imagine himself with his family back in Rwanda. Now Charles's father's brow bunched, his shoulders stooped.

Two weeks later, Konsalata and the other children returned for a joyful reunion. Once again, against all odds, the little family had survived and been reunited!

After Konsalata returned, the family made a decision to escape, leave the camp, and quietly return to their home in Uganda. When they arrived, they found their home had been destroyed and someone had been picking their coffee. They stayed with neighbors; planning to rebuild the house and move back in. A few weeks later the man who was picking the coffee from their farm told the local soldiers that Aloyizi had a son in the guerrilla army.

Early the next morning the government soldiers came and hauled Aloyizi and Charles away, along with their property, charging them with crimes against the nation. When the soldiers took someone for this reason, they would also force them to bring all of their cows and other significant resources, which they would keep if the charges held. So, they took them to a military camp, putting Aloyizi in an abandoned school and beating him so severely that he still suffers to this day. They kept Charles outside and put safety pins in his fingers and nails in his feet, trying to make him talk and give up information about the rebel camps.

A young woman whose mother was a friend of Konsalata was married to one of the soldiers. She saw Charles and knew she had to do something. She convinced the soldiers that Aloyizi and Charles were not bad people. Then Aloyizi offered them a cow from those that they had brought with them if they would let them go. The soldiers accepted the bribe and turned them loose.

As soon as they could, the family sold their remaining cows, left the Luweero Triangle for good, and took the bus to Masaka, where Fred and Specioza were living.

The war was over for them and soon would be over for everyone else. But a child can be injured in ways you cannot see.

Many years after the war, even as an adult, I would dream of running, enemy soldiers behind me coming to kill me, bullets raining upon me. I would run and run. And then I would wake up, exhausted, my energy drained.

Sometimes during the day, feelings of hopelessness, darkness, a brooding sense that "something is out to get you" would enter my mind and I would withdraw, going within to hide for a while.

It took a long time before I felt free of the war.

Chapter 3

Finding God

"For I know the plans I have for you, declares the Lord, plans for welfare and not for calamity to give you a future and a hope. Then you will call upon Me and come and pray to Me, and I will listen to you. And you will seek Me and find Me, when you search for Me with all your heart.
—Jeremiah 29:11-13

Even though I was back with my parents, the war had ended, and our whole family was now living in Masaka, many problems still remained. The war had made finding any kind of work even more difficult. Worse, we had lost everything.

In the Luweero Triangle, we lacked a home—not in the sense of a building, but in the sense of a community location where we belonged. Our family would stay in an area for a few weeks or months and then move on to another location, running away from killers, without food, water, or any real direction for life.

My father had lost all hope and dreams for his children, slipping into alcohol for relief. My mother turned to witchcraft to get answers for our family troubles. She would often make offerings to our ancestors behind the house, hoping for some kind of help. But these were gods only in our imagination. I realized they were not real because nothing ever changed. The memories of the horrors we had witnessed still haunted our dreams and shut up our songs within us.

We needed help, but no missionary came to our village. No one was available to help us with our spiritual lives when we were searching for peace and an answer to our problems. I was also struggling because I wanted to go to school but we had no money.

So, I took out my prayer book and prayed all of the prayers listed. I prayed in the name of Mary, prayed in the name of Joseph, and prayed in the name of all the other saints who were supposed to take my prayers to Jesus. But there was no prayer in that book that would take my real need to God. So I put down the book and began to pray in my own words, directly to God, that He would somehow provide the money so that I could go to school. For the first time I felt truly connected to God and I started to cry. It was the first step in my understanding of God. Things were changing in my thinking.

Not long after that prayer, Charles heard about a pastor who had a church school in the nearby village of Kyaggunda (pronounced *Cha-goon-da*). Pastor Francis Bukenya had heard the Gospel from a Canadian missionary traveling through another town, turned to Jesus Christ, and now was establishing his own mission. He needed someone to teach young children how to read and write. Charles knew he could teach the younger children because, before the war, his parents had lived in a village where the schools were good.

Our new village was poorer than where we had lived before. There were no educated people and no good schools. I was excited to find out that this pastor was trying to introduce education to children deep in rural Uganda where most people did not know how to read and write. They had lived in a cycle of illiteracy from one generation to another. I contacted the pastor for a job in his school. He decided to pay me to teach the little ones in the morning and then allowed me to attend secondary classes in the afternoon. The fact that I was offered a job to teach at my age was a miracle, but the bigger miracle was to come.

I had been working for Pastor Francis Bukenya for a few months and now I had a problem. You see, I wanted to see if I could receive pay during the upcoming school holidays. So I decided to go to see him to ask if I could have enough to get me through the school holiday. It was a peaceful Sunday morning, sunlight dancing across the hills, filtering through the banana trees as I walked to the next village. I knew the Pastor would be there preaching in the morning and then he would walk to my village later that same morning to preach. I was hoping to catch him in between.

Well, when I arrived at the village, the Pastor's wife came out to greet me. She said, "When my husband comes back he will go directly to the church. I'm also going to church now and I'm not going to leave you alone here." I thought, *I'll also go.* John, another teacher who had come with me about pay, walked up about that time. She asked us both to go to the church. As we walked, Mama Bukenya, as we called her, tried to talk us into going to church. As we got nearer, John made his get-away.

Seeing that, Mama Bukenya said to me, "Come. Let's go to church."

"No, no, not now," I answered as politely as I could. I remembered the lady I had heard on the street talking about Jesus; I really thought she was crazy. People who left the Catholic faith would go to hell; I knew that from church, so I was thinking that this lady must be crazy too.

But Mama Bunkenya said sweetly, patting my arm, "You come. Let's go."

Before I knew it, we were at the door of the church. "I'll wait for him to finish his preaching…in the classroom over there," I told her.

She said, "Charles, you need to come in. I believe that the devil is binding you from here. He's the one stopping you from going into the church."

I thought: *I know the devil. I know there is a battle between what the devil wants me to do and what God wants me to do. I can't let the devil win over me.*

Deep in my heart I questioned myself: *What kind of power does the devil have over my life? I'll show him he hasn't got any power over me!*

I decided that I would go into the church just to protest against the devil.

There was something special about the people in that church. They surrounded Charles, genuinely seemed happy that he was among them, some even hugged him. So he came back the next week and the next. Each Sunday he heard the Gospel preached although the message was not very clear to him.

The pastor was preaching from the book of Revelation and Charles didn't understand much. He had never read the Bible apart from the Scriptures the priest read to him in the Catholic Church. And there were a lot of differences in this style of worship.

Also, looking through the Bible at different verses in different chapters was not a part of the Catholic services he had attended. It seemed very different, too, because during the Catholic Mass the same things always happened at the same time. Mass was very structured. In this service, there didn't seem to be so much of a structure.

But there was something else, something important happening to Charles. After going to this new church for three weeks, Charles began to feel conviction about things he was hiding—things he wasn't telling his Catholic priest.

Father Joseph had taught his young charges that whenever they participated in the Lord's Supper without penitence Jesus would come into their hearts angry. But if they had penitence before Holy Communion Jesus would come into their hearts happy. So as a young boy he always confessed his sins to the priest to make Jesus happy.

As a boy, Charles had felt the best thing he could do with his life was to go to Seminary, to become a Catholic priest, to be near to God, and to serve the spiritual needs of other people. After all, he had been taught that the way to heaven was through the Catholic Church, and a priest played a very important role in who would go to heaven due to his power to minister forgiveness.

Now as a teenager, Charles found himself not wanting to tell the priest everything. So many things had happened during the war—things he wasn't sure he should ever get forgiveness for, things he didn't want to tell anyone, especially a priest. He began to wonder why that was necessary. Having discovered that his personal prayers to God were heard without the saints or Mary in between, he wondered about confession also. Couldn't God forgive you without another man in between?

In this new church I heard that Jesus could forgive me of my sins if I just confessed them directly to Him. I was intrigued by that. I had the knowledge of Jesus, but the Jesus I knew was so crowded—covered by Mary and the Saints. But this made sense, having a more direct relationship with God, knowing I could go right to Jesus. In March of 1984, I decided to give my life to Jesus and to confess my sins directly to Him.

When I gave my life to Jesus Christ, the weight of the past few years was lifted immediately from my shoulders. I knew I was forgiven. I knew I had connected with God in a personal way. My conversion was dramatic. Many people struggle to leave their past sin habits behind, but I found my life completely turned around.

It turned out Charles was the first person in his village to come to Jesus Christ, so he was surrounded with non-believers watching his life. They noticed he was going to church, reading his Bible, wasn't fighting with his brother anymore, and even had stopped drinking. (Drinking was a habit he had picked up trying to deal with those long, frightening nights on the roadblocks. The distilled banana beer made him feel braver.)

"You won't stay a Christian," Charles's friends started telling him. They believed Christianity was a legalistic religion, filled with rules too hard to keep.

As Charles learned what pleased God by studying the Bible and attending services, his behavior continued to be transformed. At first, Charles enjoyed the singing, the energy and joy of the people at the services, and basked in their love for one another and for him. It was a small, caring group. As Charles learned to pray and talk to God more and more, his relationship grew with God. Soon, his focus shifted from the fellowship with believers to his fellowship with God Himself.

As that happened, Charles wanted to share his new faith. He learned of the Great Commission in Matthew 28:18-20 where Jesus charged His followers to go into the world and tell others about Him. His church, under Pastor Bukenya's leading, was having an emphasis on evangelism. Everyone was challenged to go out and share the Gospel. Young people went down to the market area to tell others the good news. Usually one of them would sing and the others would share. At the end they would challenge anyone still listening with the words: "When will you get saved?"

One day the inevitable happened: they invited Charles to go with them. The only trouble was he wasn't sure he wanted to do it. It meant that everyone in the town would think he was crazy. Of course, these two guys wouldn't take no for an answer. They persuaded him to come.

As we headed down the main street that led into the market area, I slowed down. I said, "Hey, I'll meet you guys there," and then I veered off. I slipped down a back street, not wanting to go down the main street, afraid to be seen with them and labeled. When I arrived, I came up behind them. They immediately took me out front and asked me to share my testimony. Now everyone knew.

Now, my faith started causing family problems, particularly with my father. I began refusing to help my father take alcohol to his friends or to attend family parties. My father would lash out in anger, not understanding what he figured was a disrespectful, rebellious attitude. What happened to his good little Catholic boy? In the Catholic faith, it is not acceptable for someone to leave the faith—it means they are in sin and it shames the family.

It was difficult for me to explain things to my father. When I gave my life to Jesus, I completely changed. How could my father really understand that? But the more he attacked me for my faith, the more I grew in love with Jesus. There was no going back. I was telling everyone I knew about Jesus and how to follow Him.

One Sunday night my father came home from our neighbor's house swinging mad. He had found out that I had talked to the neighbor's children about Jesus. They had accepted Christ and followed me to church. They were young—thirteen, fourteen, sixteen, and seventeen. In fact, most of the church members were young.

My father yelled, "See what you are doing? I told you, what you are doing is not right! If you are a *balokore*, why are you still here? Go out and be crazy!"

Balokore is an African phrase for "the people who call themselves saved." I couldn't take it anymore. I'd had enough of the constant yelling and blaming and anger that swirled around me. So I left home.

The Bukenya family took in Charles, sharing their home with him, and encouraging him to continue to share the Gospel. During the lonely evenings after work, Charles studied the Bible and deepened his prayer life. He began meeting with other young people who had accepted Jesus Christ, and they would sometimes have all-night prayer meetings. They decided to travel, taking their newfound faith with them to share with others.

It was during these long nights of prayer, and long journeys into the towns around them, that Charles felt the Lord calling him to ministry and the mission of winning people to Jesus Christ. Telling others about the living God of Abraham became his passion. He literally would go anywhere, walking on foot through the bush, often without food or water, sometimes for several days to villages around his.

During these early days in my preaching, I used two verses. I memorized them in the King James Version of the Bible because that was all I had.

The first was John 3:16: *"For God so loved the world that He gave his only begotten Son, that whosoever believeth in Him should not perish, but have everlasting life."* I would preach most of my messages from this. I could talk a long time about that verse.

The second verse was for questions I couldn't answer. If I didn't know how to answer a question, I would look it up later, but my immediate answer would be to quote Deuteronomy 29:29: *"The secret things belong to the Lord. The Lord our God has secrets known to no one, but the things revealed belong to us and to our sons forever."*

A huge engaging smile breaks across Charles face as he remembers this verse and how he abused it.

> I loved doing evangelism and seeing people give their lives to Jesus. Our hearts were filled with joy, although few people came to Christ. We were introducing what many people called a "new teaching" so they doubted us.
>
> Now when I look back I see many people who have come to Christ due to our faithfulness to proclaim the love of Christ. Four of my brothers and sisters and some of my cousins are now Christians as well as many, many other people from those villages.

Even though he'd been kicked out of his house, Charles often went back to see his mom, always when he knew his father would be away from the house.

His mother was supportive and knew that his father exaggerated the pressure of the community to try to get Charles to renounce his new faith. Konsalata and his father's sister, Charles's Auntie Maria, went to work on his father. Six months of listening to the women—"How can you do this? He is your son, your firstborn; he is a good son too!"—and Aloyizi gave in. He called Charles home for a meeting, man to man.

"You can come back and you can be a Christian," his father said simply. "I want to see you back home."

"I have to think about it," Charles says. He recalls this with a glint in his eye and a chuckle: "I was a young man, you see, and I won!" He waited for a few days to return home just to make the point.

Chapter 4

Glad Tidings

And without faith it is impossible to please Him,
for he who comes to God must believe that He is,
and that He is a rewarder of those who seek Him.
—Hebrews 11:6

In America you have a plan for everything—for going to school, for medicine, for food, for retirement, for everything. But in Africa we have no resources; so we can have no plan. The reason people in third world countries see miracles happen is because there are no alternatives!

The Bible says that faith pleases God. Our lives are very vulnerable without Jesus. It's all about what Jesus can do! Life can be simple in the hands of Jesus. God is a God of miracles. Faith can be your walking stick.

Stop looking at your circumstances; trust in Him to do a miracle. He knows exactly what you need and when you need it. He knows your tomorrow!

As Charles preaches about faith, his words seem to come easily. But they are earned words and so there is the power of truth in them, too. It was here in Glad Tidings that Charles developed a faith-filled dependence upon God. For four years he had to believe God for everything. Just getting into Bible College was his very first lesson.

"Pastor Bukenya," Charles said to his friend one day, "I want to know about the Glad Tidings Bible College. Do you think I could go?" Charles had met a student from there who was just finishing.

"Why don't you complete an application and bring it to me?" said Pastor Bukenya. It was something Charles wanted to do, but he didn't have the money and his pastor didn't have the money either. Not only that but Glad Tidings was located in the capital city of Kampala, five to six hours and two buses away. "How will I pay for it? How will I get there? Where will I live?" He peppered his pastor with questions.

"Don't worry about the details," said his Pastor. "If it is something God wants you to do, it will happen. Just have faith." And so began a new journey for Charles, one that would take him much further than he expected.

Charles completed the application and they sent it in but he didn't get a response. The time came for classes to begin and they still hadn't heard anything from the college. So Pastor Bukenya went into action. He loaded Charles and his meager possessions onto the back of his motorcycle and took him over the bumpy, dusty, and sometimes muddy pathways out of the interior of the villages to a small town. There he said his goodbyes, sending Charles to the capital on a bus.

Charles watched him disappear out of the window, and then settled into his seat, filled with questions. He was going into the unknown from a rural area into the big city.

With his bag in one hand and a water bucket in the other hand, Charles went straight to the college. He found his way to the principal, Pastor Ponsiyano.

As he entered his office, Charles handed him a hand-written letter from Pastor Bukenya. Pastor Ponsiyano and Pastor Bukenya knew each other very well.

"Well," said Pastor Ponsiyano, after reading the letter, "come with me." He led Charles to a dormitory and showed him where to put his bag and his bucket. There were 45 to 50 beds in the dormitory. "You will start classes with the others tomorrow," he said. Then he left him to relax.

> The following day I began school. Everyone was ahead of me. I tried to catch up with the rest of them but I had challenges. I didn't have school fees and I had no money for paper or supplies of any kind. But the Principal didn't push me for school tuition; he was really sweet.
>
> Pastor Bukenya's church was under the umbrella of a conference of churches in the area. The District

Superintendant was in the area for a large pastors' meeting. He had dropped by the Bible college. I was introduced to him and I told him that I had come from his district, that Pastor Bukenya had sent me, and that I didn't have the money to pay for the college. They paid my tuition in full for two years. I was so happy for that! But it was still a difficult time.

"Why aren't you hearing me, God?" I cried out in despair one night. I thought to myself, "*The heavens have closed up again.*" I was tired. I had just washed my one good pair of pants, getting ready to go out to preach the next day. I found that I could wash them at night and dry them quickly by ironing them, so that I could wear them the next day.

While I was ironing, I was thinking. Why is this so hard? You see, many times I had no food to eat, there were holes in my shoes, I needed paper and books—I needed almost everything. "I have nowhere else to turn but You God!" I said loudly to the air around me. I was tired of the struggle. I would need food or clothing or books and I would complain to God. And then someone would send a job my way.

As soon as I was paid, I would hurry out, buy paper, and borrow notes from other students to copy and keep them for the exams. And then I would repent. I would tell God I was sorry that I doubted Him and sorry that I didn't have more faith. And then it would happen all over again. I would have a need, I would pray, I would doubt, sometimes I would get angry at God, God would provide, and I would repent again.

But at the same time I was learning. God was always teaching me. Pastor Ponsiyano Rwakatale was a great Bible teacher. When I think of him, I remember his focus was always on the Word of God, on the Bible. "God is perfect, true, and righteous," Pastor Ponsiyano taught us. "God doesn't make mistakes. If you don't understand something, God knows. Put your trust in Him." I remembered the lesson now, alone in my room, preparing to go out and preach the next day. I shouldn't be blaming God again.

I thought about what Pastor Ponsiyano told us about discernment. "When you think things and especially when you are seeking God's directions for your life, you must test the voices," he would say. "The Word of God, the Bible, is supreme. It is higher than any voice you hear, and so whatever you hear or you think God has told you, if that doesn't match up with what is in the Bible, it is wrong."

"You see, the devil likes to whisper in your ear so he can mess you up, make you think you are to do this thing or go to this place. How will you know if this is right for you to do? How do you know this is from God? How do you know if this is where you are to go? You must test it," he said. "You must look to see if it lines up with what is in the Bible. Would it please God or answer one of His instructions that He has already given you?"

I went back over in my mind how many times God proved to me that He was faithful, that He would provide for me, and that even when I was angry or ungrateful, God never changed, God always provided. *Sometimes, though, just in the very nick of time,* I thought. But that night I told God I was looking forward to seeing what He would do tomorrow. I felt light, unburdened with my questions and doubts. It was a huge change in my thinking and I fell asleep quickly with one last thought, *"Tomorrow I will share the good news! And I will ask, 'When will you get saved?'"*

There are times when you feel like God has touched your heart so much. Is this what God is telling me to do? How do I know this is true or not? How do I know if this is me wanting to do something or God who wants me to do it?

I learned during that time that if God wants to do something, He will make it clear to me with multiple witnesses. God confirms what He tells us to do through many evidences in the Bible, through circumstances, and through other Christians. They all line up.

There was something else Charles was learning during his years at Glad Tidings. Next to the Bible college was a church with an "upper room." Here several students gathered often to pray together, to read their Bibles, and to seek God's will for their futures. Irene, Justine, Steve (who is now a pastor), and many church members, including the pastor, would join the students in prayer.

This is where Charles learned to pray in a different way, imitating his friends. His prayers became less of a contest of his own will and needs set against the bleak background of his current circumstances, and more of a gratitude for what God was doing and was going to do.

Sometimes the upper room students met and prayed all night on Fridays. It was during this time that Charles learned to fast and pray for long periods. Charles says he came closer to God than ever before.

> A number of people were influenced and many things were born during that prayer ministry. A number of hearts were shaped and changed. I wish every Bible school had a prayer room. Sometimes I think when I retire I might start a retreat center where pastors and young people who want to go into ministry can come and be quiet and pray and think. Pastors who are hurting or confused in their ministry could also come. I'd like to call it *Renovare*, a Latin word that means *renewed.*

Whenever Charles was home in Masaka, between terms and during vacations, Pastor Bukenya would give him assignments to go out and to preach. For his internship, he sent him to a small village church. He had to walk for nearly the whole day into the wilderness alone to get to this church. It was a long journey.

While preaching and serving there he and some others reached out to yet another village. Nearly the whole community turned to Jesus Christ. When Charles speaks of this time, his eyes and his face light up, he licks his lips, and he glances upward. "Those were good times!" he says with gusto.

Since the third and final year of his education wasn't paid for, Charles was already working. He took jobs wherever he could, cutting grass and digging holes to make money to go to school. He went to Gaba, a nearby town on the lake, to make bricks with his hands. He also went out to share the Gospel because, as he puts it, "The people in Gaba didn't know God."

By this time Charles's relationship with his father had improved and he was supportive of his Christian life.

At long last Charles had a loving home and family to return to that offered everything he needed, but he began to feel strongly that God was calling him somewhere else. He could sense that God was preparing him for something new. But what? He began earnestly praying, asking God where He would have him serve.

> I felt like Abraham. God was saying, "Leave your people and go to a place I will show you." So I sought for direction from God. I knew that success in ministry would be determined by going to the right place at the right time. So, I had no desire to go where God did not send me!

Yet again, Charles would face a challenge in faith. While staying with his parents over his last college vacation, Charles contracted malaria.

One mosquito bite is all it takes. Malaria is a common yet deadly disease, killing up to 2 million people every year, most of them children. "To give some perspective: SARS caused fewer than eight hundred deaths worldwide in 2003, while malaria kills about the same number every six hours. For those who need to put monetary figures on this body count, the World Health Organization estimates the annual economic cost of malaria in Africa is $12 billion."[1]

Malaria's symptoms include fever, chills, headaches, vomiting, painful muscle spasms, diarrhea, and malaise. Severe malaria can cause jaundice, kidney failure, or abnormal bleeding. The parasite causing malaria can enter the brain's bloodstream— a condition called cerebral malaria—leading to delirium, convulsions, coma and death.

Malaria has a cyclical pattern and can last for months. With doctors and medicine, Charles's symptoms would have dissipated rapidly. But neither were anywhere to be found. And Charles, it seems, had a very bad case.

> At first I called out to God for healing. I had seen God heal people through prayer. I knew that God loved me and could heal me. My faith was strong. But days went by and I became only sicker. I hurt terribly from uncontrollable spasms. I couldn't eat and I couldn't even get off my bed. Finally, I could feel

death closing in. That afternoon, when there was no one around, I prayed for release.

"Father," I prayed, "I know I am near death. Deliver me from this pain, heal me, or take me home to heaven today. I'm ready to go with You now." When I finished praying, I lay there, folding my hands and feeling peaceful, waiting for death to come.

Suddenly, peace and power filled the room. I knew that God was present. It felt good to be in the presence of God. For my body, though, it was a different matter. I felt that it couldn't stay in God's presence for long.

Then God spoke, "Charles, it is not time for you to die. You are going to live. You are going to continue to pray and you are going to the nations of the world to preach the Gospel. You will go first to Gaba. From there I will send you to the nations."

From that day on, I made a rapid recovery. And I thought a lot about what God had said. I had never before considered going to other nations to preach. My plan was to become a pastor at a small church and maybe have a school like my mentor, Pastor Bukenya. This was a very different kind of thinking!

After finishing his third year of college Charles graduated, but had no money to pay his bills. On Friday Charles prayed that God would provide. On Saturday, sure enough, all his bills were paid! One last lesson from the heavenly Father—God provides!

Charles had earned an Associate Degree in Bible and Theology from Glad Tidings. In his final days he made plans to go to Gaba. He thought that ministry in Gaba would be smooth and easy. It would prove to be anything but.

Chapter 5

The Battle for Gaba

Finally, be strong in the Lord, and in the strength of His might.
Put on the full armor of God, that you may be able to stand firm
against the schemes of the devil. For our struggle is not against
flesh and blood but against the rulers, against the powers,
against the world forces of this darkness, against the spiritual
forces of wickedness in the heavenly places. Therefore, take up
the full armor of God that you may be able to resist in the evil
day, and having done everything, to stand firm.
—Ephesians 6:10-13

I take this verse, Matthew 9:35-36, as my guiding verse: "*And Jesus was going about all the cities and the villages, teaching in their synagogues, and proclaiming the Gospel of the kingdom, and healing every kind of disease and every kind of sickness. And seeing the multitudes He felt compassion for them, because they were distressed and downcast like a sheep without a shepherd. Then He said to his disciples, 'The harvest is plentiful but the workers are few.'*"

I have seen that the more people suffer, the more doors open for the Gospel. The harvest is ready in Uganda, in Rwanda, in Burundi, and in Congo. And God wants to know, what will you do to help?

The call for Charles to work in Gaba was rooted in this desire. Gaba is a suburban area just inside the Ugandan capital of Kampala on Lake Victoria. A small, solid dock juts out into a waterfront.

The banks of the lake are well-worn from the fishermen who regularly come and go. Small crates provide short term seating for those waiting to buy fresh caught fish or to catch a ride. It was then a community ruled by superstition and witchcraft.

In 1989 Charles found himself standing on a little plot of land in a small church made of mud bricks and a papyrus roof. Pastor Kasirivu and his little band of fifteen members worked very hard. People would come to the church once or twice and then never come back.

Pastor Kasirivu trained Charles to do ministry, mentoring him in many ways. But, for many years other pastors had failed to plant a church in Gaba. They would fight among themselves and go away, or they would get discouraged and go away.

Charles could see that the evil one was actively at work in this area. Why was the satanic influence so great here?

First and most significantly, traditional African religion teaches that God cannot be reached by a man because man is not yet spiritual. This logically leads to the belief that only spirit can reach spirit; therefore God can be reached only through a spirit. This belief is culturally entrenched in African thought and practice. Many in Gaba were raised to believe this.

Second, "family" in Africa includes those long dead. Family ancestors are very important in day-to-day family life. Dr. Jack Partain gives an excellent explanation of this in his article, "Christians and Their Ancestors—A Dilemma of African Theology":

> In the African view, death is not thought to end human relationships. Rather, those who die enter the spirit world in which they are invisible. Though the spirit world is a radically different world, it is also a "carbon copy of the countries where [the ancestors] lived in this life" (John S. Mbiti, *Concepts of God in Africa* [SPCK, 1970], p. 259).
>
> Deceased ancestors remain close by, as part of the family, sharing meals and maintaining an interest in family affairs—just as before death. Yet they are thought to have advanced mystical powers, which enable them to communicate easily with both the family and God. Thus they are considered indispensable intermediaries.

Throughout the day, and especially at meals, the presence of the "living dead" is often acknowledged. Small portions are set aside or spilled on their behalf. In times of extremity, expensive gifts may be offered to them to gain relief or enlist their help.[1]

As a result, many Africans, especially the poor, are vulnerable to witchcraft and divination. Their daily life is often interwoven with practices of appealing to spiritual beings. The witches seem to have a great deal of power and, after all, the demons they call upon are spiritual beings.

This made Gaba an ideal site for local African witches to set up their shrines where patrons could bring their goats and sheep to be sacrificed on a pagan altar. The blood was then used by the witches to appease the demons or to cast spells for their patrons. Of course, the meat was then eaten or sold. It was a profitable business.

In addition, since witches and others believe that divinations and spells are more powerful near water, Gaba became a hotbed for such activity. The popular name for the community became *kiryamubizi,* which means "they eat goats."

In return for their services, the witches were granted favor, given food, treated with respect. In essence they controlled many aspects of the community and opposed the intrusion of Christian beliefs and practices.

Charles was discouraged. There were only twenty people in church again! Hadn't they had forty the Sunday before when they had evangelist Alex Mitala for an evangelistic crusade? The church had worked so hard. Charles was moping. About that time, Peter walked in. He and Charles lived in a small room.

"Peter, I'm so tired. I'm so tired of preaching and no one is coming to faith. I just can't live this life. We need to start praying instead of just visiting!"

And so they did. The small band of young Christians began to have days of fasting and prayer, to seek the face of God to break down the power of the devil in their community.

They decided to meet on Friday nights because that was when the witches met next door. Sekajja's shrine, one of the largest in the city, was only ten meters away from Gaba Community Church.

On Friday the shrine was full of activity. The drums beat loudly, reaching a crescendo every now and then while the witches chanted and danced, calling out their incantations and offering their sacrifices. As the drums grew louder, the little group of Christians would pray more earnestly.

Sometimes, as they prayed, calling upon God to send His power down to protect those in the community from the witches and to stop the devil from reigning in the hearts of the people, the drummers grew tired. They would want to stop and go eat. And the witches' songs grew sadder. Their demons were not answering their call.

At other times, though, the witches would celebrate; their demons were present. It truly was a war. The church continued to pray, at times fasting and praying for several days and nights at a time. The witches' victory drums droned less often.

Sekajja grew angry. He called upon the demon powers to stop the little group of upstarts. He cried through the fire and the goat's blood, calling upon the names of the most powerful demons he knew, begging them to injure the Christians, to do them harm, to take them over. He cursed them all by name.

The small group of believers suffered from spiritual attacks. They experienced unusual bouts of doubt, fear, and anger. They also experienced countless instances when things went wrong, often tempting them to stay away from the next prayer meeting. But they persevered.

One morning Charles found the remains of a sheep left on the property where they met to pray. The witches were becoming desperate.

Then, not long after that, the World Bank gave a grant to Uganda's National Water Corporation to build a new water pumping station. The Water Corporation decided to build their new station and the housing for their workers in Gaba.

Where exactly? They chose the area along the water where most of the witches lived and worshiped. The National Water Corporation compensated them for their land and asked them to leave immediately. In a very short time all of their homes were destroyed along with seven of the witches' shrines.

After the witches left, the heavens opened up in the community and people started receiving Jesus Christ as their Savior and coming to Gaba Community Church. The church began to grow and whole families were coming to Christ.

Whenever you mess with Satan's territory, though, you can expect him to mess with yours. And he gets personal.

With increased activities on the lake came government soldiers assigned to patrol the lake's borders. The leader of this patrol didn't like the church. Furthermore, the District Secretary of Defense hated the church and was very suspicious of what they were doing.

First, Charles and many others in the church were young. In fact, it was a movement led by young people converting other young people to a new religion that many didn't understand.

Second, the fact that the church's young men and women were meeting at night also didn't bode well. You see, the band of prayer warriors was not giving up; there were still witches in the area; Sekajja was still right next door.

A few questions in the right ears—What were they up to? Were they plotting against the government? Were they out to take over the region?—was enough to create a problem. These reports would have to be investigated. Soldiers have autonomy to do whatever they feel is necessary to break up any suspicious activities, and many times they do not pay penalties for behavior which can be quite brutal.

It was Thursday evening and they were praying in the church, six men and three women. Security operatives, the local lingo for the soldiers, came and demanded they go with them.

> They marched us to the business center and began caning us, a physical punishment consisting of a number of hits with a thick wooden cane. One soldier took away one of the women and raped her. Along with this physical and mental punishment came a stern warning not to pray at night again.
>
> Later that night, in my room alone, the horror of what had happened weighed upon me. The beating had been terrible, very penetrating. "Lord, I don't understand. Why did they come and beat us? Why didn't you protect us? What will happen if we pray again?" I complained aloud.

And then I thought, *There have been so many times when I had no food and You fed me, when I had no clothes and You clothed me. You have always been faithful, bringing me through so many trials. I can't keep on doubting what You can do in such hard times! I have to trust You, because You are trustworthy.*

During this nighttime of wrestling I lost my fear of death. I knew we had to go back and pray. I made up my mind that when I did, I would trust God for whatever would come next. I went to see the others the next day, telling them that I would return to pray, and urging them, although they were afraid, to return as well. "We cannot disappoint our God," I told them.

On Friday we returned to pray. Pastor Kasirivu, who had been out of the city the night before, and many more people were there this time. It was 3:00 a.m. when at least forty security operatives surrounded us.

"Why are you here tonight? We warned you and told you not to do this again. Leave the tent now and follow us," one of the soldier's yelled at us.

I told my friends, "They have guns but we are not leaving!" Then I turned to the soldiers and said, "If you want to kill us, go ahead. It is better for us to die in the house of God than out in the streets. We are not leaving!"

One of them pointed his gun at me, grabbed me and began tugging me out, tearing my coat. I sat down on the ground with a thump.

"I am not going to walk out. If you want to take me out, you will have to carry me. I know what you did to us yesterday. This night I am not going with you."

I turned to my friends and said, "Don't be afraid. Don't give in. Let's pray."

Then Charles calmly led them in a prayer for the soldiers around them. The others sat down as well and began to pray loudly for the soldiers and for the other lost people in their community. Peter, the shepherd of his flock, went out with the soldiers to try to negotiate with them, and to explain what they were doing at the church at night. The soldiers took a head count and told the church members: "We will be back in the morning to take you to the local court. Do not leave."

They were true to their word and returned early the next morning. The Pastor found himself before the Kibuye Police Post. After answering many questions, they were commanded to stop praying during the night. Pastor Peter stood his ground, insisting that the remaining witches worshiped at such hours.

"Why will you allow them to have loud night parties in the community but stop us from praying?" he asked. "Many evil activities are going on around here at night and we feel God is calling us to watch the community in prayer," he explained.

They returned to regular prayer meetings the following Friday night. During the course of the week, Peter went to the police. He asked about their constitutional rights in relation to freedom of worship. He used the law and the constitution to argue their case. The Secretary of Defense decided to let them continue prayer at night. The soldiers stopped coming. And remarkably, the soldier who raped the girl came back to ask for forgiveness.

Fifteen Christians stood the test and persevered, praying for their community, willing to sacrifice even their lives. And Gaba began to change.

> Witchcraft and poverty tend to go together. They are sisters. They are relatives. Poor people get caught up in it and it blocks the blessings of God to the people.
>
> In the Bible, God told Abraham to come out from his people, out from the gods of the Chaldeans and Uriah and to head for the land of Canaan. In his homeland there were many false gods, including in the city of the Tower of Babel. So, when God wanted to bless Abraham, He brought him out, away from his false gods. And then He began to bless Abraham. This is what happened in Gaba. As soon as the evil one was defeated, God began to bless the area.
>
> The Defense Officer who persecuted and supported the closing down of the prayer meetings came to the Lord and his children attended the churches' school, which now educates more than 600 children, many of them poor and orphaned. The witchdoctor next door saw a decline in his clientele. Eventually

his evil business collapsed and he became a poultry farmer. He sold his property to the church; God miraculously provided the funds for the purchase.

Gaba Community Church continues to grow. In 1996 they broke ground for the construction of Gaba Community Church Building, officially dedicated June 18, 2000. It is a mother to more than eighty churches around Uganda. Missionaries have been sent out to Rwanda and Tanzania.

In 1990, God gave Pastor Peter and his friends a vision to reach the world through equipping young men and women for leadership. That ministry became known as Africa Renewal Ministries. It has grown to be a big international organization with ministries to children (sponsoring more than 5,000 Ugandan children), pastors, families and communities throughout Uganda.

In 1995, Mrs. Irene Kasirivu started a children's choir. The Mwangaza Choir has ministered in the U.S.A. and Holland in various high level events including the Dove Awards. This choir also has been blessed to be featured in songs with accredited gospel artists Michael W. Smith and Nicole C. Mullen.

Gaba Community Church today has an average attendance of 1,500 youth and adults and more than 1,000 children on a given Sunday.[2] The village of Gaba is completely transformed and is busy spreading the good news throughout the region and elsewhere around the world!

During this time of growth, Charles was busy doing what he learned to do under his pastor at home, including traveling with small groups and preaching the Gospel in every area they could. He was the assistant to Pastor Peter, preaching and teaching, and developing his passion to help children with their education and their spiritual needs.

Little did Charles know what was coming next.

Chapter 6

To the Nations

Ask of me and I will surely give you nations as your inheritance and the very ends of the earth as Thy possession.
—Psalm 2:8

And you shall receive power when the Holy Spirit has come upon you and you shall be my witnesses in Judea, Samaria and even to the remotest part of the world.
—Acts 1:8

One day I went early in the morning alone to the tent, where we now had church services, to pray.

"Charles, I want you to go to England." The thought just popped into my head. I remembered when I was sick with malaria that God had told me He would send me to the nations.

But I argued with this thought a bit. *I haven't ever traveled anywhere more than 300 miles from here. Why would I go to England? I don't know anything about Europe.*

Another thought. *"I will break the pride of the British people. They are living in a spiritual valley. I want you to go."*

Even though I didn't go right away, I began to pray for the English people, that God would lift them out of their spiritual valley. The more I prayed, the greater my burden to pray for them became. For four years I prayed but I was also busy building the church in Gaba, preaching, and working.

One day while praying I read Psalms 2:8, "Ask of Me and I will surely give the nations as Thine inheritance, and the very ends of the earth as Thy possession." I went back to my room and posted a big sign that said, "God has given me England!" I believed my prayers, asking God for the transformation of England, would make a difference.

I began to feel God had something more for me to do, especially in the area of preaching. So I began to ask God, "What is next for my life?" In order to get clarity, I decided to take a break for seven days to pray and fast. I stayed with a pastor friend in Kampala in a small room.

During those seven days God made it very clear to start working on going to England. "Without faith it is impossible to please God, because anyone who comes to Him must believe that He exists and that He rewards those who earnestly seek Him" (Hebrews 11:6). Faith begins by envisioning the impossible.

God's dreams come with the power to complete them. But you will not find your dream until you spend time before the Lord. God is not in a hurry. Most of us pray "popcorn" prayers. With God you must take your time. You must allow Him to wake you up and give you His dream. Until you do, you are like a sleeping giant.

It became clear in my heart and my mind that going to England was what God really wanted me to do. I gained a sense of peace and direction. And then, when I pursued that direction, each step I took, God blessed me so I knew I was on the true path He had for me.

During this time Charles was also working for Compassion International as a project director. With this money he was able to rent a large house where Peter, his younger brother Fred, associate pastor Emmaus, their worship leader Grace, and Godfrey all lived together. Anyone who earned anything would bring it to help pay expenses.

When he came back from his fast, Charles went to his room and posted an even bigger sign, "God is going to give me England!" He was going to England somehow. The time for prayer was over; Charles went into action and started asking people "How do I get to England?"

He found an address of a church in England and wrote to them, asking them to sponsor a trip to England. They wrote back.

The letter said, "We cannot invite you because you don't belong to our denomination."

A short time later, Peter found an announcement about a Christian leadership seminar in England. So he challenged Charles to write to them for an invitation to come. He soon received an invitation.

While Charles got his first passport easily, getting a visa was more difficult. It was hard for a young person to get a visa to Europe at this time because many people were trying to migrate from Uganda to Europe and then to America.

"To me, getting this visa was a real puzzle," says Charles, "I just didn't see how that was going to happen." He went to the British Embassy, letter and passport in hand. He was told to come back at two o'clock to pick up his visa. He received a six-month visa, no more questions asked. This was extremely unusual at the time.

Laughing at the memory, Charles says with a shrug of his shoulders, "I still don't know where I am going! And I have no money. But I have my passport and my visa. So now I started praying for money."

Within a short period of time, Charles was invited by Steve, one of his friends from the upper room, to speak at his church. Part of his message that day was to tell the congregation about his vision to go to England. A business woman gave him $150 after that meeting. Other church friends and close friends helped as they could and soon he had almost enough for his plane ticket.

The last person to give him money was a lady who had come to speak at Gaba. She knew Peter and had heard through him about Charles and his trip to England. She prayed about it and God seemed to impress her with a specific amount to give. So with money in hand, she asked Charles, "How much money do you still need?"

He told her $250, an enormous sum to Charles, a poor Ugandan preacher. She said, "That is exactly how much the Lord put on my heart to give you," as she handed him the money!

> So now I had a visa, a passport, and a plane ticket, but I still didn't know where I was going. I remembered that my Bible College principal had a son, Steven, who lived in England. I

went to see the principal to ask if he thought his son could help me. Well, he didn't have Steven's phone number and, anyway, overseas calls were very expensive. While he was telling me this, his phone rang. It was his son Steven calling from England. He agreed to pick me up from the airport."

I was on my way to England!

Charles enjoyed the flight as a great adventure. But he did have a bit of trouble with the escalators. The first time he encountered one, he put one leg on and, well, that was awkward. Then getting off was "troublesome," as he puts it. So, he practiced until he was comfortable with them.

Steven was at the airport to greet Charles. Other than Steven, Charles only had two other contacts: a friend had given him an address for a family in Hemingford Grey in Cambridge, and Phyllis and Ian Hassan, who had visited Gaba and lived in Northern Ireland.

After he attended the conference, Charles asked God, "What do you want me to do? Lord, where am I going to preach?" He knew he could stay in London and minister to the African immigrants there. Those churches were giving him many opportunities. But again, he bowed to God's direction. God said, "Leave London. Go to where the English people live."

And so he called the family in Hemingford Grey. And through the help and generosity of a Jamaican he met at the conference, he found himself sitting on a Sunday morning in a 700-year-old English Anglican church named Saint James in the small English village.

I was the only black man in the church so I prayed quietly that God would open a door for preaching to these people. The family I was staying with introduced me to Kerry Dixon, the assistant minister of the church. Kerry was too busy to talk with me that day. He did come by their house to see me, however.

A few years ago, Kerry told me that after that first interview he just decided to accept my story, that I had a burden from God for the English people, and thought to himself, "If he messes up, I can fix it."

At the time, Kerry was preparing for a two-week mission of evangelistic effort in the school, in the pubs, and in a disco hall. He had invited a well-known English evangelist, Don Egan, to come and preach. Kerry contacted him, telling him about Charles.

Don Egan remembers this: "I really felt the Holy Spirit instruct me to befriend Charles and to invite him to Stowmarket after we finished at Hemingfored Grey. Then while I was at Hemingford Grey the team had lunch together every day and I began to get to know Charles. I remember thinking that I would someday go to Uganda with him."

During the next two weeks, Charles taught the church how to intercede for each other and shared with them his experiences in Gaba—how to fight a spiritual battle and how to deal with a demonic environment that is hindering people from coming to Jesus Christ.

Don invited Charles to come and stay with him in Stowmarket. During that time he says he and Charles shared their testimonies and their vision. There seemed to be many similarities even though they were from very different cultures. A true friendship developed as they traveled around; Don connected Charles with other churches around the UK on this first trip and subsequent ones.

Along the way Charles witnessed a real outpouring of God's Spirit. "It was like the original days of the book of Acts. They were very open at that time to the things of God," he recalls. Miriam, a woman at that first meeting who was living on welfare and had a sight disability, determined to support Charles. She would support his ministry significantly for a number of years.

After some time, while Charles was in England working with Don, he remembered his friends from Northern Ireland and felt led to contact them. They invited him to Ireland, sending money for his fare by bus and boat from London through Scotland and across the Irish Sea.

It was on one of these first trips that he met Ronnie and Joyce Finlay, who became supporters and prayer warriors. Ronnie still prays for Charles every Saturday, something which means a great deal to a praying man like Charles.

Charles experienced Northern Ireland at a time when many people were hurting. He remembers meeting many lovely people, but he could see the demonic environment of divisiveness equivalent to what was happening in Rwanda between the Tutsis and Hutus.

While Charles was there in Ireland, the killings in Rwanda increased, culminating in a mass genocide. There are many similarities in the two situations. There was a long standing history of animosity between Protestant and Catholic ethnic communities in Northern Ireland just as there had been between the Tutsis and the Hutus in Rwanda. There had been many skirmishes resulting in deaths on either side, especially in Londonderry where Charles preached in a Presbyterian church.

Some of the worst fighting occurred there when bloody riots broke out in 1968. British troops were brought in to restore order, but the conflict intensified as the IRA and Protestant paramilitary groups carried out bombings and other acts of terrorism. It was a guerilla warfare carried out with guns and bombs instead of machetes—but it was still neighbors killing neighbors and many innocent suffered.

This continuing conflict, which lingered into the 1990s, became known as "The Troubles," and between 1969 and 2001 more than 3,500 people were killed as a result, most of them innocent civilians.

The impact of "The Troubles" on the ordinary people of Northern Ireland was also similar to the struggles experienced by the people in Rwanda. It too produced psychological trauma— the stress resulting from bomb attacks, street disturbances, security checkpoints, and the constant military presence. There was chronic unemployment and a severe housing shortage. Fear and distrust permeated the societal fiber. Government soldiers often stood by while attacks happened or were incriminated in some of the violence.

Also, normal interactions and friendships with people from the opposite side of the religious/political divide were nearly impossible. In a report in 2007, the high rate of suicide in Northern Ireland was linked to "The Troubles" as well.[1]

Charles had studied Saint Patrick and his walk through Ireland in Bible College and so for him it was exciting to be there, visiting the old castles and actually walking where this great man had confronted witchcraft, so prevalent in Ireland at the time. It seemed to Charles that there was still a pervading sense of evil, and he preached love and unity of the brethren and talked often of keys to successful spiritual warfare.

While in Ireland, Charles experienced many new things. One evening the doorbell rang at the home where he was staying. He opened the door to find a group of masked children, calling out in loud voices at him. The masks were hideous and he immediately thought to himself, *These must be demons!* He stood up straighter, pointed his finger at them and fearlessly bellowed in his most authoritative voice, "I command you in the name of Jesus Christ to be gone! Demons, release these children in the name of Jesus!"

The matron of the house, rounding the corner, came to his rescue, calming the terrified children and handing them each some candy. Once they were gone, she explained to the much bewildered Charles that this was a yearly holiday where children dressed up in masks and costumes and went house to house begging for candy. They were calling out the greeting "Trick or Treat!" as was the custom.

Returning to England, Charles continued to preach wherever Don arranged for them to go. But the day came when he needed to return to Africa.

Don says, "On his last night in Stowmarket, I pressed Charles to tell us how he would live when he returned to Uganda as he had given up his job to come to the UK. He seemed to have only faith (which is a good beginning). A few of my friends wanted to support him so we set up a fund called Uganda Partnership. It was only a small fund but it helped ease Charles into ministry on his return. It also helped us raise funds for his airfares to and from England."

Charles remembers receiving money from England in plain envelopes. He said he was always amazed when they got to him in Uganda, unopened.

Don Egan and Charles forged a friendship that has led to a lifelong partnership and both of them remember the days of revival in the UK and in Africa. Of those times, Charles usually says with a sort of melancholy in his voice, "Those were good days!" You can tell he relishes the memories. They saw many miracles and many people come to Jesus Christ in both Africa and the UK. Thousands of lives were forever changed by two men obeying God and asking the question, "When will you get saved?"

It wasn't long before Charles found himself traveling to Ireland and to England, living between two continents and three countries—splitting his time preaching to the London African immigrants, traveling and preaching throughout England with Don Egan, occasionally returning to Northern Ireland, and ministering in Gaba.

During this same time some other very important connections began to form that would prove to be important not only for the church in Gaba, but also for the coming ministry in Rwanda.

Gerald Seruwagi, on the charter board of Africa Renewal Ministries, is a Presbyterian friend who had worked with Charles on many projects in Gaba. Gerald had traveled from Uganda to go to Bible College in Texas.

There he met Dr. Randy Draper, who was the Senior Pastor of Maranatha Bible Church. Pastor Draper took him in and he became a part of the Draper family. Gerald decided to bring Pastor Draper and his wife, Darlene, to Uganda on a mission team with Dr. Bill Thomas. Dr. Bill is an African American world evangelist who lives in France. After that trip, Dr. Bill came to Uganda many times; he also introduced the church in Gaba to the Luis Palau team.

Dr. Randy Draper became a father figure for the entire church team in Gaba. His wife became like a mother for Charles, Pastor Peter, and Gerald. Pastor Draper ordained Charles and provided financially for a lot of his needs. Charles says, "They were the first door of God's blessing to lift Peter and the entire ministry in Gaba from the ground. The first child sponsorship in Uganda came from the Maranatha Bible Church."

Charles now found his network of support reached from England to Ireland, across Africa and to the United States.

He was indeed preaching to the nations!

Chapter 7

Passion and a Dream

O Lord you will hear the desire of the meek;
you will strengthen their hearts, you will incline your ear
to do justice for the orphan and the oppressed,
so that those from earth may strike terror no more.
—Psalm 10:17-18

They were running, screaming, dying, a whole family wiped out in moments, murdered by their neighbors with machetes, or shot by soldiers—their bodies picked up, loaded onto a truck and unceremoniously tossed off a high bank into the Akagera River.

This river originated in Burundi, forms the Rwanda-Tanazania and Tanzania-Uganda borders, flowing finally into Lake Victoria.

During the 100-day Rwandan genocide, precipitated by years of repression, ethnic division, and political manipulation, at least 800,000 people were slaughtered by their friends and neighbors.

Charles remembers hearing about the corpses floating down the river. His family and friends stopped eating fish when they realized the fish were eating the corpses.

According to a report compiled by the Parliamentary Standing Committee on Unity, Human Rights and the Fight Against Genocide, chaired by Evarist Kalisa, tens of thousands of genocide victims were washed down the rivers of Nyabarongo and Akagera, both tributaries of Lake Victoria, and landed at different shores of East Africa's biggest lake. The bodies were later buried at six different sites in Uganda.[1]

What happened to create such a situation? The trouble began in 1916 when the Belgians chased the Germans out of Rwanda. At that time there were three tribes occupying the land. The first tribe was the Tutsis (Batutsis), who herded cattle and were tall and quite light-skinned. Next were the shorter, darker Hutus, who farmed. Then there was a small pigmy tribe.

The Belgians enlisted the Tutsis, although they were in the minority, to help them develop and exploit a vast network of coffee and tea plantations. Elevating the Tutsis allowed the Belgians to avoid war or the expense of deploying a large colonial service. But over the years this created a smoldering resentment among the Hutus.

When Africa began to shake off Imperial Rule in the 1950s, Rwandans followed suit. The Tutsis began to demand freedom and ownership of the plantations. At the same time, Gregoire Kayibanda created a Hutu social movement based on the program outlined by the Hutu manifesto of March 1957, which he helped to author. In September of the same year he was sent by the "white fathers," Catholic priests in Rwanda, to a journalism course in Belgium.

When Kayibanda returned to Rwanda in September of 1959 he created the party called Parmehutu.[2] As a final ploy to remain in control, the Belgians backed an uprising led by Kayibanda that sought to slaughter or drive out the Tutsi elite.

Some 130,000 Tutsis fled into the neighboring countries of Burundi, Uganda, Congo, and Tanganyika. There they formed small insurgent groups, calling themselves *inyenzi,* or cockroaches, with the aim of restoring the Tutsi monarchy. Raids across the border gave the newly elected President Kayibanda an excuse to begin a full-out purge of Tutsis throughout Rwanda, with local groups killing some 10,000 and driving tens of thousands more into exile.

In 1973, Major General Jenvinal Habyarimana, a Hutu, toppled Kayibanda in a coup d'état and began a twenty-year dictatorship. It led to a degree of stability in Rwanda that was envied in the volatile Great Lakes region. But the expulsion and persecution of the country's Tutsis sowed permanent seeds of discord.

Slowly, the Tutsi diaspora became a force to be reckoned with. Fueled by the continued oppression in Rwanda and harsh treatment at the hands of their reluctant host countries, the diaspora finally coalesced into the Rwandese Patriotic Front. A small but highly effective military and political movement, the RPF proved capable of engaging and defeating the French-based Rwandese Government Forces.[3]

At the same time, Habyarimana's government faced great challenges and he began losing his grip on the nation. The population in Rwanda had grown from 2 million in 1940 to 7 million in 1990. Drought had blighted food production and a sharp drop in world coffee prices cut farmers' income by half.

On top of that, there was growing resentment about Habyarimana's corrupt dictatorial rule, and pressure was growing internationally for election reforms.

As a response, Habyarimana's regime began authorizing anti-Tutsi propaganda, filling the airwaves with Hutu power propaganda and helping to spread a climate of fear and hatred. In addition, relying on the Hutus culture of obedience, he began to arm local militias and organize death squads.

The President's death, when his plane was shot down over the capitol on April 6, 1994, resulted in an immediate call to exterminate the *inyenzis*. The genocide that followed was caused not by ancient ethnic antagonism, but by a fanatical elite engaged in a modern struggle for power and wealth using ethnic antagonism as their principal weapon.[4]

Nobody knows who shot the rocket that took the plane down, but that very night the presidential guard instigated a 100-day killing spree, starting with Tutsi political figures in high places. Within hours, recruits were dispatched all over the country to carry out a wave of slaughter. Encouraged by the presidential guard and radio propaganda, an unofficial militia group called the *Interahamwe* (meaning "those who attack together") was mobilized. At its peak, this group was 30,000 strong.

Soldiers and police officers encouraged ordinary citizens to take part. In some cases, Hutu civilians were forced to murder their Tutsi neighbors by military personnel. Participants were often given money, food, or promised that they could appropriate the land of the Tutsis they killed. Those who refused to participate were also murdered.

The day after Habyarimana's death, the RPF renewed their assault on government forces. Finally in July the RPF, still led by Paul Kagame, captured Kigali. The Hutu-controlled government collapsed and the RPF declared a ceasefire.

The end of the killing spree and the routing of the Hutus precipitated a family crisis for the Buregeyas. Of those who perished in that killing spree, Charles's mother lost her brother, his wife, and all of their children, with the exception of one girl who was in Burundi at the time. Charles's father's sister lost all of her children.

For many years Aloyizi had dreamed of going back to his own country, where a man could live on his own land and enjoy a sense of well-being. He loved this land, the land of a thousand hills, and remained very patriotic. He never found purpose in Uganda, since most Ugandans did not welcome the Rwandan refugees, and there was little economic opportunity for the men.

Yet the conflict of war, never finding a community where they could put down roots, and the loss of their coffee plantation all took a terrible toll on Aloyizi.

Although he planned and worked for a better future for his children, he couldn't provide it for them. He greatly missed his homeland, often thinking of the peaceful hillsides dotted with farms, the fields of coffee and potatoes laid out it neat squares near the thatched homes, the lowing of the cattle at dusk ready for milking, and the banana trees whose leaves give shade and rustle quietly in the cool breeze.

Aloyizi also greatly missed the people greeting one another along the roads and at the market, exchanging news of family and friends. He missed walking along the roads and among the hills. He missed the feeling of permanence, of being home. He longed for peace again and to be back rebuilding the life he once knew.

So when the genocide of the Tutsis ended, Aloyizi returned to Rwanda. Konsalata, however, was afraid and refused to go with him.

> It was 1995, a year after the genocide, when I found myself on the way to find out what was happening with my father. I was hoping to work for reconciliation between my mother and father, but that trip proved to be a catalyst for a call from God and a life-long passion and dream. God used my father to lead

the rest of us back to Rwanda. He broke the power of fear in us.

I convinced my family that we must join my father in Rwanda, to at least go and check things out. The bus was hot and rickety, dust swirled around us.

As we crossed the border into Rwanda, my mother and I both stared out of the windows, lost in thought. People got out and kissed the ground when we crossed over the border. But as the bus rolled onward the more depressing it became—signs of the genocide were everywhere. There were RPF soldiers and UN troops on the ground everywhere as well.

I thought about the Luweero War and the government soldiers, but the RPF soldiers were kind to the returning Rwandans. If they had been threatening in any way I would have taken my mother out of there. But knowing there were still killers around, we gained confidence from the RPF soldiers who often said, "We are here to protect you."

We arrived in Kayonza that night where we met my cousin, Francis Gakuba. He and I had grown up together although Francis was much younger. The following day he took us to where my father was living.

Francis later became an influential helper to Africa New Life Ministries. It's amazing how God has used Francis Gakuba in my life. He has dynamic negotiation skills and can negotiate very hard deals. He has many connections, mostly gained through his avid love of soccer and even more determined support of soccer in Kigali. He can often be found at the stadium, selling T-shirts, mobilizing people to go for the games, and supporting it all with fundraising.

He has helped us purchase most of our property. You have to negotiate for property in Africa and the owner can lie to you about prices or even if they really own the property. You need someone who is very in the know.

The following day Francis took us to where my father was living. He was alone in Kayonza, a small farmland community where a lot of people had been murdered. He had bought some property and was helping to rebuild the community. The area had been deserted and was just now being repopulated.

The signs of death were everywhere. Bodies smelling everywhere, many unburied even now—a year later! Orphaned children, widows, homeless people milled about aimlessly...it was chaos.

At night everyone was supposed to go into their houses to leave room for the military to patrol, but there were many children who had nowhere to go so they slept on the streets.

It reminded me of a biblical scene. Just imagine the Jews returning to Jerusalem and the whole city is deserted, the walls are broken, the houses and roofs have holes, the doors have shifted from their location. It was just like that but worse. This touched my heart profoundly.

The suffering in Rwanda seemed to be endless. The results of the massive killings had been so thorough that in many communities there was no family left to bury the dead. Many of those who were responsible for their deaths had fled when the new regime finally gained control of the country.

Over two-thirds of the nation's people were refugees in other nations. The government was overwhelmed with the sheer number of dead. Even now, well over fifteen years later, many of the dead, although now buried in a more dignified way, remain unidentified. Charles and his family have never found any trace of their loved ones.

Charles left the area where his parents were living and headed to the capital. He had heard that some of the younger people he grew up with were now in Kigali.

"When I arrived, I didn't know where I was going to stay," recalls Charles. "I just wanted to make contacts. As I was walking I saw the man who had given us the tent we used for worship in Gaba, Leo Rucibigango. I stayed with him. He was there to plant a new church in the city. I would go to the church to pray with them at night."

During the day Charles was out investigating the city, meeting people, seeing what was happening. In Kigali, Charles was particularly struck by the number of children who were left without parents or family to care for them.

The lucky ones were located in make-shift orphanages run by NGOs (non-governmental organizations). They housed incredible numbers of children, straining their resources to the brink. Relatives, family members, even neighbors now had extra children to try to feed. Many children had no one left in their family and so had nowhere to go.

As well, hundreds of children were living on the streets of Kigali. And there were very few opportunities for any of the children to go to school. Most of the teachers, professors, community leaders and community developers had been murdered or had fled to other countries when the RPF regained control.

It's estimated that 20 percent of the Rwandan population were murdered and somewhere around two million Hutus fled to Zaire (now called Congo) and to Tanzania, Uganda, and other places. In the wake of those terrible days, vulnerable, innocent children were suffering. Because of his own experiences growing up, Charles knew their pain.

> When I left Rwanda, I left with a new burden. I kept thinking, *How can I get back and help those children? What can I do for the people of Rwanda?* I began to pray earnestly for the people, particularly the children, of Rwanda. There was no way I could leave those people in that same situation. I knew I had to do something; I knew God would want me to do something.

Back in Uganda, Charles was introduced to Sammy Tippet, who came to do a crusade all over the eastern part of Uganda. An evangelist from San Antonio, Texas, Sammy Tippett likes to go to difficult places that have been damaged by war, and preach the life-changing Gospel of Jesus Christ.

This seemed to be an answer! Charles shared with him his passion to preach to the people of Rwanda. So, from Uganda, Charles and Sammy went to Rwanda. In 1996, they did three crusades in the span of five days in Butare and Kigali.

As they traveled about, meeting the people and sharing the Gospel, Charles's burden grew to reach out to the needs of the genocide survivors, especially the orphans. Hundreds of people came to Jesus Christ during those crusade meetings.

Every time we would finish one of these events, I would watch the people leaving. I knew we were going to a safe place, but I would think, *How about the kids? Where will they sleep? What are they going to do tonight?* God totally broke my heart and I decided to help rebuild Rwanda. I began praying for support. A fire had been lit in my heart.

After returning from those crusades, I told Peter, "I'm giving you two years here and then I am going to Rwanda."

That was a reasonable plan, but my friend Gerald Sseruwagi began to encourage me to come to Reformed Theological College in Kampala where he happened to be teaching. Gerald is a well-educated man with two master's degrees. He argued that if I got more education, more doors would open for me to go and preach because people like to listen to an educated evangelist. He told me that I really needed to have an accredited Bible college degree. He also told me that I shouldn't be concerned about spending the next four years to prepare for the next forty or four hundred!

Gerald was head of the department of theology and felt that African Christianity lacked spiritual depth because so many of its pastors were untrained. He said African Christianity is a mile wide and an inch thick. Gerald was very persuasive—his arguments were strong.

As I prayed I felt that Gerald was right. *But*, I thought, *I'm preaching in England, I'm preaching in Gaba, I'm 27 and I want to go to Rwanda.* So what did God tell me to do? God told me, "Go back to school...and get married!"

"I don't need any more training," I complained to God. "I already know how to preach. But I do need a wife!"

God knew, however, that Charles was going to do more than preach. God knew he was going to be a ministry leader of a large organization, work with government leaders, deal with staffing, budgeting, purchasing, building and promotions. He would need *much* more training.

Of course, Charles didn't know that...yet.

Chapter 8

Florence!

The LORD is my light and my salvation; whom shall I fear?
The LORD is the strength of my life; of whom shall I be afraid?
—Psalm 27:1

In February 1989, the same year Charles received a call from God while on his deathbed, Florence Mutamba had her first encounter with the Holy One.

Florence was raised Catholic and was very committed to the Catholic Church. But one evening as she was walking home from school, one of her teachers happened to be walking with her. He shared with her about what it meant in the Bible to be born again.

"Florence, do you love God?" he asked her.

"Yes!" Florence replied, "That is what going to church is all about. That is why we go to church."

"If it is all about loving God, then it must be a personal relationship. You know, love is a person-to-person thing, isn't it? And so it is more than just going to church."

Florence nodded, understanding the difference for the first time. Her teacher continued: "The Bible says the way you can have a loving relationship with God is through Jesus Christ. It says we must be born again first. Jesus himself told this to Nicodemus, a religious man who went to church a lot. To be born again, according to Jesus, is to have your spirit born. When you accept that Jesus Christ died on the cross for your sins, paid the price for your sins, we say you accept Christ.

"Before you accept Jesus Christ, your sins are still counted against you and keep you from being close to God. He is holy and cannot bless sin or you as long as that sin is there. To accept Christ is more than just going to church, though. You must give your life to Him and be willing to listen to what God tells you to do. That is how we truly love God.

"When you receive Jesus Christ, He says you will know His voice. You will hear God speaking to you and you will know that it is Him. You will have a difference in your spirit because it will no longer be dead in its sins and unable to hear God. Instead, it will be alive to God!"

Florence replied, "I want to hear God speak to me and I want to show my love to Him."

That night she gave her life to Jesus. As she puts it, "Right then an idea came up into my mind: '*You never, ever forget about this decision. It is a special thing you have done.*'"

In recalling this she puts great emphasis on the *never, ever.* "It was God speaking to me for the first time!" she says, her eyes gleaming.

As a child, Florence wanted to have shoes, to be clean, and to have pretty clothes. She would often get into trouble because she didn't want to take care of the family cows and goats. She was living in western Uganda in Isingiro in a village where there was no school. She knew that if she could go to school she could make a better living for herself and wouldn't have to look after smelly cows anymore!

Their neighborhood church was evangelical so Florence was also growing in her knowledge of the Bible. Because she was voted to be a leader in the fellowship for student Christians, she had to read her Bible a lot and they also prayed together. She learned a lot during this time from the godly people around her. She says, "I asked God so many questions. I learned to read the Bible. I really prayed and sought His face."

And then came "The Hill," her most difficult challenge. In this part of Uganda, there was very little water, no farms, just bush area. The families would combine their cows and take turns taking care of the animals. Each day one person would be assigned to take the cows up into the bush on a hill nearby. This hill had more vegetation for the cows to eat.

In the sixth grade now and the firstborn in her family, Florence was the one who had to take care of the cows when it was their turn. "Be careful on the hill," the other villagers would warn. "Keep a careful watch! There are many large snakes up there."

African snakes are the most dangerous in the world and many of the worst kind occupy this region of Africa. There are the puff adder snakes whose venom when released in a single bite is incredibly dangerous and usually fatal.

Then there are the black mambas, which are considered one of the most deadly and aggressive of all snakes, especially when they are disturbed. And the gaboon viper loves the equatorial region of Africa, has the longest fangs of all snakes, and the quantity of venom those long fangs deliver is almost always fatal.

The African rock python is the largest snake in Africa and the third largest in the world. They can grow up to 25 feet long and weigh more than 200 pounds. It is non-venomous and so relies on stealth to get close to its prey. Once it closes in, it bites, latches on with its teeth, and then quickly coils around its victim. Suffocation follows quickly. Then the prey is swallowed whole. Larger python have been known to attack children; mostly they eat birds, crocodile, gazelle, and other mammals.[1]

Imagine being in the sixth grade, alone, with no shoes, on a rocky hilltop, knowing there are snakes all around you. Florence says that hill drew her closer to God. She would pray a lot, asking God to keep her safe from the snakes.

Many times, she says, she would be sitting on a rock and an idea would occur to her: "You'd better leave this spot. There could be a snake." She would get up and move only to see a huge snake passing by, sometimes just next to where her feet had been. She came to know the Lord was watching over her, answering her prayers.

Other times, Florence would be hungry or thirsty and ask for strength. She remembers one particular afternoon when it was extremely hot and she had no water, nothing to eat, and there wasn't any fruit she could pick. She was standing on a rock behind a bush, trying to stay cool.

She began to pray, "Lord, I am going to ask of You one thing. If You do this one thing I will do two things for You. If You give me an education so that I can come out of this life, I'm going to serve You with all of my life. Number two," she said,

"I'm going to tell it to everybody. I will tell everyone about You." It was a serious statement, she says, one that she has never forgotten. The very spot is still etched into her memory, so deep was her commitment.

Right after this prayer, Florence's father decided to send his daughter to school. He sold one of their cows and made arrangements with friends in Jinja, where he had grown up and lived for a time. This family became guardians to Florence, who helped them around their house. In this way, Florence was able to finish school.

Then one day her guardians announced they were moving to Kampala. Florence fasted and prayed and sought God's face for guidance. She says she remembers when God spoke to her, telling her that this family would be a blessing to her. And so she determined to go with them to Kampala to see what God would have for her there.

The very first Sunday in Kampala, Florence met Winnie. Winnie asked her many questions, most she couldn't answer, and Florence realized she really didn't know what she was there to do. She refers to Winnie as "an angel from God" because it was through Winnie that she found out about Reformed Theological College. Florence had a deep inner desire to serve God, but she didn't know until this conversation with Winnie how it would ever come to pass.

When Florence heard about the college, she knew this was why she had come to Kampala. But no one was interested in helping her; she had no friends in Kampala and no one to turn to for support. So, she decided to go and meet with the college director to see if she could work at the college and pay her way through. The way she puts it is, "I didn't have one single coin to pay."

On the way to the office, Florence says she took Jesus with her, talking to Him out loud as if He were standing beside her. She remembers telling Him in the hallway just before she entered the office, "Jesus, please go in before me. Convince him for me, Lord." She told the director all about her desire to come to his college and that she was willing to do any kind of work so that she could pay for it. When he agreed to let her come, she says she stood on her feet, raised her hands, and thanked God for the great opportunity to achieve her dreams! She was soon working as an administrative assistant for the college and enrolled in classes.

During those first few weeks, Florence realized there wasn't a church in the community. So she and some other students began to meet on the campus, bringing neighborhood children with them, visiting the families, and sharing the Gospel. Florence began preaching on Sunday mornings from the pulpit. Her theological understanding was limited and so she didn't know that many Presbyterians and Koreans (who also attended the college) would not sit under a female preacher.

All Florence knew was that she had a great desire to share Jesus with people. Regardless, the little church began to grow. Soon more students from the school were coming since they couldn't afford transportation on Sundays back to their home churches.

Just as the church began to grow, Florence found herself doing all of the work herself. The original group of students helping her had all moved on. She struggled to keep her school work going, to do her job with the college, and to prepare for Sundays. It was a "great work!" she says. So she did what she always does in difficult times, turning to the Bible and beginning to pray for help.

She prayed from Ephesians 3:20: *Now to Him who is able to do exceeding abundantly beyond all that we ask or think, according to the power that works within us, to Him be the glory in the church and in Christ Jesus to all generations forever and ever. Amen.*

This became a favorite promise. "This Scripture will always be my encouraging verse," Florence says. "God used it to give me hope for great things for God and to push me to believe God for greater things than what my human abilities can do."

It wasn't long before those prayers were answered by a new student, Richard Lwanga. She says, "When I asked Richard Lwanga to come and help me, he hesitated." But someone else, who didn't know Florence, also approached him, also telling Richard that Florence needed his help and that she felt impressed by God to talk to him about it.

"Richard couldn't hesitate any longer!" says Florence. "He came to help me and it was such a relief to me in many ways."

Although Florence and Richard enjoyed church ministry, they needed help—the church was growing so fast they couldn't keep up. They began praying and asking God to move the professors to step in and help.

One morning during the service Florence saw them coming in. Eventually they took over the entire church leadership, helping to steer their growth.

About this time Florence remembers watching the news one day. They were showing the genocide and the bodies floating on the river. The church where she ministered to children had regular five o'clock prayer meetings for all of the staff. Florence remembers bursting into tears as she was praying about the children in Rwanda. She knew those children were starving and she wanted to help them.

In 1995 Florence's parents had gone back to Rwanda, sending her a message. She didn't know where they were but when two of her best friends, Jovia and Jully, said they were going to travel there to find their relatives, she knew she had to go too. *If I don't go with these ladies,* she thought, *I won't get to go.* She had a little money, but it was her tithe.

Florence agonized over what to do. She told her friends she couldn't buy the bus fare. She gave her tithe to her church as she always did. Then, a man who was their friend said he would pay for her ticket, but on the morning they were to leave he was nowhere to be found.

"I have to get on this bus," she told the bus driver. "My best friends are going to Rwanda and I have to go with them. My parents are there but I don't know where. I have to go and find them. I don't have the money but I have to go."

"Okay," he said. "Stand here by the door; if there is one spot left you can go."

She waited anxiously. There were two spots left! As soon as she got settled, she was startled by a knock at her window. It was the man with her ticket money. He gave her the money through the window. Because she already had one passage free, she used the extra money for meals for herself and her two friends.

"My goodness," she remembers, "I was so excited I preached the Gospel on the bus, I gave a testimony, and I finished by saying, 'You people need to know Jesus!'"

When the bus crossed the border to Rwanda, people were kissing the land. Florence noted the date and the time she stepped on the land of Rwanda for the first time. People all around her were rejoicing, crying, happy to be back in their land.

In Kigali, Florence was shocked. The streets were full of dirty, miserable, hungry, sad faces of children everywhere. By six o'clock everyone would be back in their homes. As they traveled back at night, she would see kids, lying down together, preparing to sleep, young little kids huddled in groups all along the streets.

"That picture has never left my mind," she says, her eyes widening with quick intensity, her head nodding a definitive exclamation mark.

Florence was able to find her sister, Peace, in Kigali but did not find her parents until a later trip. When she came back to Uganda she told everyone she was going back to Rwanda to help with the suffering children.

"I knew that it was going to happen; I felt like God was calling me there. But I thought I would be a missionary through the Bible school. When that didn't happen, I tried to work with the Red Cross but it didn't work out."

God had put a dream in her heart, but little did she know where it would lead her.

Chapter 9

Reformed and Married

*Delight yourself in the LORD and
he will give you the desires of your heart.*
—Psalm 37:4

My first day of arrival at Reformed, I met Florence. She was working for the school, and on this day, helping new students get enrolled.

As soon as I saw her, God said, "This is your wife."

I wasn't into the business of getting to know girls because I was a little bit conservative and very shy, so I prayed for nine months.

We didn't talk until September or October. But every day I would see her and I would say "Hi." I was praying and making decisions. I didn't want to be driven into a relationship.

We were around each other a lot and I would listen to her. I found out that her parents originally came from Rwanda. She was a pretty girl, she was leading and praying and serving, and she had a vision to go back to Rwanda.

To say the least, I became more and more interested!

Florence remembers this too. She says, "In December I was working in the Bible school and Charles had come to check in. He started to school in January of 1997.

"When we met, although we really didn't know each other at all, somehow our hearts were like a magnet to each other. I was shy but I wanted to be around him and I didn't really know why.

"We would run into each other in small groups having lunch and talking. We never really dated. You know, I was encouraging the girls in my charge at church, the young teens, not to focus on men and here I was thinking all the time about this one man. I would ask God, 'Why do I love this man?'"

At this time, Florence was a church leader, holding ladies Bible studies, overseeing the children's ministry, and taking care of many other duties. She wanted to be a good example to those in her charge.

As she says this, Florence looks up and shrugs to make her point clear.

"Charles was really what I wanted. I had written what I wanted in a man in my journal three years before this, and he matched everything I had written!

"One morning Charles was sharing with the other students that he wanted to go back to Rwanda and work with children. Every time he would talk about his plans I would be thinking, *Hey, that's my vision too!*

"So I began earnestly praying, asking God to show me if this was the right man. Two days later Charles asked me out."

Charles interrupts her and, almost rising off his seat, says, "And you said no!"

Florence grins and says, laughing, "I was busy organizing something," and hurries to add, "but I came to your house to visit you."

"With a girlfriend!" says Charles as the frustration of that visit touches his voice again. Turning toward me he says, "You see, I wanted to know if she had a boyfriend," he tells me, cocking his head sideways. "I wanted to make a move knowing where I was going to land."

"Well," says Florence, "I was taking steps to see if God was confirming this or not. So, now I was praying even more: 'Really, God, I want you to lead us!' I thought God was confirming it. Charles was planning to go to England and said, 'While I'm gone let's pray seriously about our relationship.' He was gone for three months."

Charles says, "I took her picture and looked at it again and again. People were asking me if we were getting married. 'She is my friend,' I would say. When I was in England, I wanted to make a move forward when my emotions were not involved. I thought God was indicating she was the person. And so I called her on the phone."

Florence says, "When Charles went to the UK, I seriously wanted to know what I should do. I was in a full-time ministry with my church, I had a good job, and I was going to school. So I decided to fast and pray for a whole day, and during that prayer I was asking God to really confirm our relationship.

"I prayed to him, 'Lord, You are real, You change not, You are always the same. In the Bible we see You speaking through the prophets and the angels. I want to see something supernatural confirming our relationship.'

"I got up from my prayer and went back to my desk. It had stormed in the area and our phones were not working. We were not able to call out or to receive any phone calls because the telephone lines were broken all over the area. At the desk I was met by a South Korean woman who was visiting our college. She didn't speak English very well.

"She asked me, 'Why phones not working? Phone not working—why?' I had been praying and crying so I didn't want to look her in the eyes.

"She said again, 'Why not working?'

"I picked up the phone to show her it wasn't working and Charles's voice said, 'Hello, Florence?' It never even rang.

"I said, 'Charles?'"

"I think you are to become my wife. I think God is telling me this, so we need to talk about a wedding," Charles told her with a sort of urgency.

"I was trembling, sweating, so shocked!" remembers Florence. "Even though I had been praying for this very thing, I was so amazed. I thought, *God is down here with me in the office!*

"'I have sent you an angel, Florence,' I could hear God saying. 'What more do you want?'"

As Florence hung up, she offered the phone to the South Korean visitor, but it was dead. Try as she might, she couldn't make another call out that day.

As Florence tells this part of their story, Charles nods his head with a short little nod: God was on his side. Of course she said yes!

"So we started talking right then about our wedding and that was the topic of our days until we got married," Florence says.

73

Charles says, "When you marry an African girl you must get permission from both sides of the family. As a Christian, I believe you need several witnesses before you get married: the witness of the Spirit, the church leaders, your friends, and your mother. I took her to my mother and the same day my mother said yes!"

When they visited with Charles's parents, his mother entertained them, gave them a Fanta (a real treat in Rwanda), and showed off her new daughter-to-be to the neighbors.

"They live in an open community," Charles explains. "Anyone can come in any time. They help each other so every one of the ladies came to see Florence. This was great news for my mother; she was really excited about it all!"

Florence didn't like the inspection from the neighbors, but she endured it. Her nose wrinkles when she talks of it now, as if she's smelling rotten bananas.

"My dad," says Charles, "was mostly quiet but he asked Florence, right before we left, about her parents—Who was her father? Where did they live? Were they in Rwanda?—the usual questions."

Florence smiles a charming smile. "He's my good friend now," she says. "He and I talk on the phone a lot. He cried when my father died. They were friends."

Charles says, "Now I had to visit her parents. This visit is really important. The father asks you who your father is, where do you come from, where do you work, all of those kinds of things. I was scared to death. You see, you also have to pay a dowry, usually four or more cows was expected for an educated woman, and I told Florence, 'I don't have cows.'"

The big day came. Charles hired two motorbikes to take them to Florence's home to discuss the wedding with her father. "You ride behind the drivers," Charles says to me, explaining why they had to have two bikes. "Florence went first and then I followed."

"Most students tried their best to hire a small car," says Florence, "but we had the motorcycles." Florence is still frustrated they didn't hire a car that day.

"I didn't want to live out of my budget. I just wanted to be myself," explains Charles. "It's a little bit different when you go to visit your father-in-law," says Charles. "I sat there quiet. I didn't know the Kinyarwandan language and I didn't want to make a mistake. They gave me a cup of milk; this was an accepting gesture and is very traditional. And then of course they asked questions," explains Charles. "He asked me questions like who is your father, where do you come from, where do you work, when do you want to get married, those kind of things. I was very nervous, scared to death."

Florence interjects, "When things are out of his control, he gets very nervous."

After a groom presents himself to the father of the bride, he must discern if the atmosphere is accepting. If so, the groom is expected to offer a dowry. If the father doesn't like the groom or dowry, he tells his daughter, "Don't bring that man back," and that is the end of the relationship. Charles, being a missionary, and really quite poor at the time, didn't have the usual dowry and offered only two cows. His father-in-law graciously accepted.

Florence says, "My dad was very easy. Some men would do it like they are selling and buying. My dad understood. He was nice."

The motorcycle returned for Charles at the appointed time and he left.

"My friends from England and Ireland gave me money and I was able to pay for two cows," remembers Charles.

In Africa, weddings involve the families and the community so there is a ceremony in the bride's family home. People drink and dance with traditional dances. But Florence boldly requested a Christian introduction of her own style, with prayer and a pastor-led service. The worship team even came over.

"We had a fabulous wedding," Florence says. "Being a pastor in Africa, you tell everyone that your wedding is coming so we had about 700 people there. We were so shocked when we saw our picture in the national newspaper," she adds, her eyes twinkling. She said, "God was with us." They were married in a Christian church wedding on November 14, 1999.

A few days later, Florence found herself on a trip to England with Charles. For Florence it was a grand honeymoon, filled with new experiences, some a delight and some challenging. She had never been away from Africa and flying was a big shock.

They got off in Brussels and had to catch their next plane. There wasn't much time to make the connection. "Let's go!" said Charles, "Let's run!" And so she hurried after him, dragging her carry-on and her jacket and then...they get to an escalator.

Charles says, "Just jump on!"

But Florence can't do it. Then she sees a man fall as he gets on. "I can't get on this machine. I don't want to try new things! I am not entrusting myself to this machine!" she says, her eyes flashing. She digs her heels in.

But Charles persists, "Let's get going. It's safe. It's okay; it's not going to hurt you."

Florence looks at me, smiles, and says, "Soooo, we jumped anyway." Whenever she wants to stress a point, she stretches out the vowel. I understood this to be a significant moment for them, their first newlywed conflict. In the end, they missed their connecting flight. Fortunately, there was another flight not too much later.

When all was said and done, the newlyweds had a wonderful time in England. They had a few weeks to themselves and then Charles started preaching. They also attended several conferences, but often they had all day to enjoy being tourists before the evening services. To this day, Charles always lets Florence speak for the first few minutes whenever she accompanies him on his trips, a practice he began during this very first trip.

This underscored for Florence the changes that were coming and she found herself wondering. She had her own strong ministry with children and with young women. She knew Charles was a very strong person and that God was going to do things through him, but she didn't know how she was going to fit into all of those plans. How was she going to be able to have a happy marriage with him?

As Florence was visiting around in churches, she met a Nigerian woman who was a minister. She asked if she could pray for Florence. She said, "You are going to leave your ministry. God says you are going to have different goals. You will need greater faith. I see you as a Sarah, following her husband. You are going to leave your country and travel for the Gospel."

Florence was shocked because her father had wanted to call her Sarah, but her mother didn't like the name.

The woman continued, "Florence, you are a woman of faith, but you have to follow your husband even when things seem hard. He will reach a point when he says 'We will do this.' You will want to ask him, 'Why are we doing this?' But God says 'Pray and follow.'"

"I never forgot what God spoke through that lady," says Florence. "All that she told me, we have seen it come to pass. This laid a foundation for our ministry and a happy marriage."

Next they traveled to Northern Ireland and Scotland and took the boat across the sea. Florence recalls this with a good bit of giggling. She says, her eyes growing wider to show the emotion, "I really had a surprise the day we set sail for Ireland. We went to the docks and wandered into this area where there were some stores. Charles stopped to play a coin-operated motorcycle racing game. I kept waiting and waiting for him to finish."

Finally Florence said, "Shouldn't we get on the boat now? Aren't they going to leave us?"

Charles said, "Florence, look one step behind us." A whole group of people were sitting in neat little rows of chairs. Then he said, "Go and look through that window over there."

Florence laughs. "And I could see the ocean, miles of ocean; we already were on the boat! I said, 'Okaaaay.'" She tells this with a bit of embarrassment in her inflections.

Florence also says she got sick while they were away. Back in London, Charles became concerned because Florence wasn't getting better; he thought she might have malaria. As it turns out, Isaac, their first child, was an Irish surprise.

When the newlyweds returned home, they rented a house and stayed with Pastor Eliseé Rugambarara, a friend they had made the previous year. During this year, while Charles was writing and praying about his vision for Rwanda, Eliseé would pray with him and listen to him. They became great friends.

"He owns a vision of New Life Bible Church," says Charles. This is the first church they began in Kigali. Pastor Eliseé became its executive pastor and is, according to Charles, a wise man, soft with people, a good Bible teacher, very trustable, and very objective.

He is also a powerful leader. "When he makes up his mind about something, it is sometimes hard to change," says the forward-thinking Charles.

Charles particularly appreciates Pastor Eliseé's ability to help others get along and has nicknamed him "ombudsman."

By the time the year was over, they were a rock-solid team. But their vision wasn't big enough yet. God had more in store for them.

Chapter 10

America? You've Got to Be Kidding!

Trust in the Lord with all your heart;
do not depend on your own understanding.
Seek His will in all you do,
and He will show you which path to take.
—Proverbs 3:5-6 (NLT)

"**T**wo words come to mind when I think of Charles," says long-time mentor and friend, Dr. Tim Robnett.

"The two words are faith and obedience. Whenever he would come to me with a goal or an idea, I would tell him, 'Charles, you need to do this,' and then he would go out and do it. He'd just go charging out in faith and make it happen whether he had resources or not. And he did that over and over again."

When Charles met Dr. Robnett, it was an act of obedience. Charles was back working in Gaba and was about to leave for Rwanda. His heart was so burdened that he would pray for hours and weep for Rwanda. Out of this zeal and passion, he felt he simply should go. But God told him that night, "Don't go to Rwanda." He couldn't shake it so he decided to obey the Holy Spirit and drove to his church in Gaba instead.

Dr. Tim Robnett served with the Luis Palau Association for many years. His ministry included directing international evangelistic festivals in twelve nations, overseeing conference and evangelists training sessions in many other nations, and coordinating missions in India and Africa. He did all of this while also training seminary students at Multnomah Biblical Seminary in Portland, Oregon.

At about this time, the direction of his ministry took a big change and Charles Buregeya was to receive the benefit. That same year Dr. Robnett had become the director of Luis Palau's Next Generation Alliance.

The sole purpose of this ministry is to equip a new generation of proclamation evangelists. So, he and a good friend of his from the Luis Palau ministry team, Dr. Bill Thomas, traveled to Kampala, Uganda to investigate evangelistic ministry opportunities for Next Generation Alliance evangelists.

This day they were guests of Pastor Peter Kasirivu, the pastor of Gaba Community Church, but there wasn't anyone there who could translate into the local dialect. Then in walked Charles, obedient to God's change of plans, so now he was able to spend the day translating for them.

"After the meeting I had the chance to visit with Charles for a few minutes, not long," remembers Dr. Robnett. "He expressed his desire to go to seminary one day. I chatted with him about Multnomah Biblical Seminary and he said he would like to come visit me there. I responded, 'You get to Portland and I will host you.'"

Something clicked in Charles's mind. At this time, Charles says he had a great battle within himself, struggling between going to seminary and going to Rwanda.

> Clearly God was telling me to go to America thousands of miles away even though I wanted to go to Rwanda only ten hours away. A few months later I had an opportunity to go to England to preach. At about the same time, Maranatha Bible Church in San Antonio, who supported my ministry, called and invited me to come and attend a Missions Conference. Suddenly I was going to America!

As he stepped off the plane in San Antonio, Charles felt the ten dollars he had in his pocket. He wondered again if going to Portland was really what he was supposed to do. He had sent most of his money home from England already, deciding that he had to take care of his family first and that God would provide for him as he went. It was a practiced response.

Now Charles's faith was about to be tested yet again!

While Charles was in San Antonio, Pastor Draper introduced him to America, taking him to a large shopping center. He bought him a nice suit, a tie, shoes, a shirt, and, as Charles put it, "He just cleaned me up and Americanized me." Pastor Draper also provided several other preaching opportunities for Charles.

One day a phone call came from Florence. "Charles, we have been robbed!" The night before in Rwanda it had been moonless and very hot. Florence had moved from the master bedroom, where she and Charles usually stayed, into the room with her baby because her uncle was expecting some company. She woke up because of the extreme heat.

She fell back asleep only to wake up when she heard a sound. Then again, she knew a visitor was coming. Not hearing anything more, she lay back down only to wake up moments later to the presence of a man towering over her. Not understanding what was happening, she asked, "What do you want? Are you the guests who are coming tonight? Is there something you need?"

"You want to help us now? Okay, we want money now," said the man with a smirk. Florence began to realize what was happening. She heard the sounds of many people moving things, taking things out the door, looking through their things. Her eyes grew wide and she grabbed for some more clothing. She heard Charles's brother Godfrey waking up. They were taking the rug he was sleeping on. The teenager woke with a cry and one of the robbers hit him, knocking him back down to the floor, yelling, "Don't look at us!"

And then she heard her uncle's muffled cry. "Put up your hands, old man," she heard the voice bark. They covered him with his bedding so that he couldn't see them, ransacked his room, and even took his watch. He sat very quietly under the blankets, not wanting to make a sound so as not to be killed. He knew that attracting attention, making noise so others outside the house might hear, could get them all killed. The robbers had machetes.

Florence said to the man in her room, "We don't have any money, but take whatever you want. We don't have any money, but I have a checkbook. I can sign it for you. You can take anything you want." They didn't want the checkbook but they took most everything else.

The robbers worked fast. Soon they had the computer, the babies' clothes and toys, the rugs, the cell phone, the sewing machine, everything from the kitchen, everything from their closets, stripping the house clean in a matter of minutes.

Florence was very calm, giving them instructions where to find her uncle's keys to the car. She remembers thinking it was really lucky she wasn't in the master bedroom. Usually robbers come to the master bedroom first because the person in the master bedroom is considered the owner of the home. Many times that person is murdered.

One of the men asked for the keys to the other car. She told them, "I don't know where those keys are. That car hasn't run in years." It was her car. She was hoping they wouldn't take it because it did look beat up and old. They believed her.

Florence knew it was important to stay calm and quiet. But Florence couldn't help herself. She remembers praying loudly, "God protect us. God keep us in the name of Jesus."

"Are you a Christian?" one of the men asked.

"Yes, I am," she said, and prayed again loudly, "In the name of Jesus, keep us safe, Lord." As Florence retells this story her sentences pick up speed and you can feel the tension. As they were taking everything from the baby, Florence complained silently to God, "How can you allow this to happen to us?" Isaac, six months old, was left with only the little night shirt he was wearing.

Romans 8:29 was also running through Florence's mind. "And all things work together for good for those who love the Lord and are called according to His purpose." Yet she wondered what good could come out of this robbery.

As she remembers the situation, Florence tells me, "You know that in your life there is something you always think about; it is the most intimidating thing you can think of and it frightens you. Getting robbed was that secret thing that frightened me. Now this fear is gone."

Charles is a family man, so this was a very severe situation for him. "I'm coming home," he told Florence as soon as she finished the story over the phone.

"No!" Florence said. "It's done. What can you do now? This is the work of the enemy trying to stop your mission trip. You have to go to Portland," she told him.

She quickly adds, "I didn't know that he would be successful there. I really didn't think he would. But I knew that he had to go and find out."

Friends in San Antonio gave Charles some money and he went shopping for her. A friend was traveling to Uganda on a mission trip, so Charles sent new things to Florence from the church in San Antonio. Florence remembers receiving a yellow dress with matching yellow shoes. She giggles as she remembers them and says, "I was a queen!" Isaac also had wonderful new baby clothes. Their church in Gaba also helped them.

Thanks to Florence, Charles was more resolute than ever.

> The devil is very tricky. He was trying to stop me from going on to Portland. But because of Florence's bravery and insistence, I phoned Dr. Robnett. I simply said, "Here I am in America; I am coming to Portland."

"Great! You arrange travel to Portland and you can stay with me and my wife and I will show you around," Dr. Robnett remembers saying. Not long after this Pastor Draper bought Charles a plane ticket for Portland and gave him some additional pocket money. Two days later Charles called Dr. Robnett again from San Antonio and said, "I will be arriving on Thursday night on a Continental flight."

"Okay, I will be there to pick you up," Dr. Robnett told him. "I had no idea what I was going to do with Charles. But I sensed that God would provide," remembers Dr. Tim, as all of his mentored students called him.

Charles went to Multnomah and interviewed with the school officials. Academically he qualified, but the challenges of coming to America to seminary included raising money, a lot of money. As an international student you have to prove that you have twenty thousand dollars in order to go to an American university. Charles met this the same way he always met challenges: he prayed. The school offered a 25 percent discount because he was coming from a very poor situation.

I refer to the time between my trip to Rwanda with my mother and actually moving to Rwanda as "the waiting room." It was really a painful time. God sent me to seminary in Portland. I knew I had to finish school. God knew I was a man of action and that I needed more training in the area of waiting. However in the School of Waiting, God didn't waste time. God never wastes time, even when we can't see what He is up to!

It was painful for me because I saw the need and the pain in the Rwandan people—experiences very familiar to me because of my past. God had given me the dream and now He was providing the training suitable for the dream. God knew what was ahead and He knew also that I would need help; I would need a strong network of ministry supporters.

You can hear an edge in Dr. Robnett's voice as he talks about Charles. It's a proud father's voice mixed with admiration and godly respect. He watched the next two weeks as God opened door after door for Charles.

"It was an adventure in faith as I introduced Charles to seminary professors, school officials, friends, and local pastors in Portland. Day after day, Charles would share stories of answered prayers, new friends made, and his official acceptance into Multnomah Biblical Seminary. We also worked with the seminary to establish a Uganda Scholarship Fund," says Dr. Robnett.

He continues: "In a matter of a few weeks Charles was admitted to the seminary, funding channels had been established, and people in Portland were already beginning to support Charles with prayer and finances. Charles was also used of God to create a new awareness for the needs in Rwanda. I was amazed at how quickly the Holy Spirit was providing and guiding each step Charles was taking."

On that preliminary visit to Portland, Charles met many of his key partners at a small group Bible study. Attending this group were Rob Bauer and Tony and Serena Morones. This small Bible study group was instrumental in providing finances for Charles and Florence to come to Portland and also in the early formation of Africa New Life Ministries. Tony and Serena have served on the board and Rob and Lisa Bauer have led many mission trips to Rwanda. Alan Hotchkiss, involved in the small church plant where Tony and Serena met, joined the team a bit later as the executive director of ANLM. Before joining ANLM, Alan, also a graduate of Multnomah, worked for the Luis Palau Association.

Other financial support came from friends in Texas, as well as pastors and mentors Charles had already met through his work abroad and in Gaba.

Once the funding was secured, there was one more hurdle… visas!

> I was still struggling against the idea of more school and so I decided that if we didn't get visas to go to America, especially for Florence and the baby, we just would go on to Rwanda. Visas were not easy to secure at that time; it was more difficult if you didn't have family or business ties, and sometimes they would ask for land titles or proof of citizenship in Uganda before they granted one.
>
> Of course I had no land at this time. Most people would lie to get their visa, but Florence and I prayed that if God wanted us to go, we wouldn't have to lie. Our interview was short, we were not asked any questions, and we were quickly given visas.

Within less than a year, Charles was back in Portland with Florence and Isaac, his young son. He was starting classes and making many new friends. After just one semester, Florence, thanks to money already collected for ministers from the Uganda Seminary Scholarship Fund, also enrolled at Multnomah Biblical Seminary. Charles was majoring in the area of Ministry Management, and Florence was pursuing a degree in Family Ministries.

"Both of these programs were under my guidance at Multnomah," says Dr. Tim, as Charles now calls him, "so I had the privilege to work closely with Charles and Florence in their academic programs. But as much as they studied, doing very fine academic work, they worked just as hard at founding African New Life Ministries."

Charles and Florence experienced many new things in their time in Portland. On one particular occasion, Dr. Robnett was invited to enjoy a foursome on the golf course with Charles, Reid Saunders, and Brad "all for Jesus" (Charles's nickname for him because he would say that all the time).

"I have my clubs," Charles said, beaming, as they all met up that beautiful morning. "I got them yesterday at a garage sale."

"I should have known then it was going to be a long day," says Reid.

"Have you ever played golf before?"

"No, but I am ready!" was the answer from this let's-just-do-it African.

"And there we were," Reid says, "over an hour later still on Par 4, with Charles hacking away at his golf ball and the rest of the golfers playing through. It was a very long day."

As the legend goes, they were nearing the end of the course and Charles's ball was near the green. "All for Jesus" was on the green lining up his putt when out of the blue, Charles took a full swing at his ball, instead of chipping the ball as anyone else would. His ball makes a beeline straight for Brad's head, causing him to dive into the green. Charles, realizing his mistake, calls out, "Oh, my brother, I am so sorry!"

Reid, enjoying telling the story, adds "We had to explain that this was about unity of the brethren, not killing the brethren," and then laughs. It's a good-natured story among a small band of friends, all actively being used by God to spread His Gospel.

Other significant experiences for Florence and Charles during their years in the United States included the birth of their other two children, Jonathan and Sara. There also were driving lessons, as well as many new things to eat, many choices to make, and much work to be done.

Through it all, Charles and Florence never lost their passion for the children of Rwanda. So it was with great excitement that Charles began working on one of his last seminary assignments. He was asked by Dr. Robnett to develop a ministry plan and was guided through that process.

In 2008 Dr. Robnett was standing before the newly built Dream Center in Kigali, the church of his student, Pastor Charles. Charles introduced him in part by saying that he was his mentor and good friend. Then he said, "He helped me put together a master plan for Africa New Life. Whenever I get confused I just go back to this plan. It keeps us on God's path." It was a very meaningful moment for Dr. Tim, one he still cherishes today.

For five and a half months, Charles and Dr. Tim worked on the plan. As I talked with many of his friends in Portland, I discovered that many of them had been sounding boards for this plan—giving advice, listening, and encouraging Charles. Of course, many others contributed, too. It was an unusually gifted group. Serena has financial acuity. Dr. Robnett has an equipping, discipling mind. Fred Katagwa went on many fact-finding missions to Rwanda. Florence made her own contributions to the plan, as well.

Most of all, Charles was dependent on God. Charles says he simply wrote down what he felt God was leading them to do in Rwanda. As he worked he prayed, and he felt God was speaking through this paper and guiding him in every step about the things he wanted to do in Rwanda.

> After developing the plans, I could not sit back any longer. I was working in the seminary kitchen, washing plates and cups and cleaning up to earn money, and every time I threw away food, I thought of all of those kids out on the streets who were starving. I wished I could ship it to them somehow. I went home and told Florence that we would go to Rwanda over the summer break and see what needed to be done.

Dr. Robnett remembers those days this way: "I had the privilege to reflect with Charles on what God was calling him to do and also to discuss how he was going to do it. We brainstormed together the possible names for the ministry and came up with African New Life Ministries. From this master plan we formed the ministry corporation, board of directors, and launched ANLM.

"As a mentor to Charles I can say only that I listened, encouraged, and attempted to connect Charles's dream with resources to fulfill the dream. Then I went about my life and

Charles, full of faith, charged out into the world to discover how God would use him to build ANLM.

"Faith is a relentless energy provided by God to move His vision forward through his obedient children. Charles and Florence are two of those obedient children."

Exactly! Charles charged out—a man of action, a man with a burning passion, a man with a new well-planned vision and full of faith—but God had something more planned for him.

Chapter 11

Africa New Life Begins!

Let us think of education as the means of developing our greatest abilities, because in each of us there is a private hope and dream which, fulfilled, can be translated into benefit for everyone and greater strength for our nation.
—John F. Kennedy (1917-1963), thirty-fifth president of the United States

---

When you go throughout the whole world, the needs of the poor are overwhelming. I found out this important truth:
You cannot change the whole world,
but you can change the world for one!
That is where Africa New Life began.

You see, as soon as our third year was over at Multnomah, Florence and I flew back to Rwanda. During that trip over the summer we did not go to start a ministry. We went to see what God would lead us to do in the future. But when we arrived, the need was so big I just could not keep waiting and seeing.

In my plan back at Multnomah, I had written the basis of my vision for Africa New Life Ministries, which is God's heart.

The heart of God is a two-handed approach. When you pick coffee, you have to use two hands. What one hand can reach the other cannot. If you don't use both hands you cannot reach all of the coffee.

For me, these hands are the proclamation of the Gospel and acts of compassion. On the one hand, children need to have food, clothing, shelter and education. They need to know they have a future. They need to feel safe and secure. With sponsorships we can do this for many children.

On the other hand, you must speak the word of God. I didn't see any way we could give children food, clothing, education and shelter—and then see them go to hell. That would be unfair. That's injustice really. That's hiding real life from the people. Real life is eternal life. In John 10:10, Jesus said, "I have come that you may have life."

God provides all the material things for our comfort while we are still here. We can provide material things that bring physical comfort, but there are also things we can do to bring spiritual comfort. We can teach a child that they can meet their mother or their father in heaven and connect with them after this life. This brings them spiritual comfort.

After being back in Rwanda for a few days, visiting his parents' home in Kayonza, walking the streets of Kigali, and seeing thousands of children hanging around with no place to sleep but the streets and nothing to do all day, Charles could stand it no longer.

Charles turned to Florence and said, "I know you have some money. You've been babysitting children in America. Would you mind if you gave your money for us to start a preschool, a place where these children could come in and it would be some sort of humble beginning?"

Florence had heard his passionate, tearful prayers for Rwanda. She also had a dream to help the women and children in Rwanda. She knew that he had a burning passion and it was one that she shared. But…she had been saving this money for a new home, a place for their family to live when they came back to Rwanda permanently. It had been so hard to leave all of her belongings behind in Uganda when they went to America. She had sold or given away all of her new china, all of her pretty pots, her first stove, their new couch hand-made by a friend, all of her beautiful wedding gifts—everything a young bride wants for her first home.

Part of her knew God would provide, but the other part of her wanted to keep those nice things. Now, she was asked to give away the money she had worked so hard to save for starting over. Yet Florence didn't hesitate. She said, "Yes!"

"And so," Charles says, with a wide smile, leaning toward her, "Florence became my first donor!"

Next, Charles contacted his brother Fred Katagwa. He said, "Fred, we are starting a preschool for the orphans and I want you to come. I need you to take pictures of the children and collect information about them. We want to get sponsors."

Fred had been living with Charles while he was in Gaba and had finished his education there. Fred came to see Charles in Gaba. Back home he was not able to go to school; there wasn't enough money. Still, Fred's plan was to return home, but Charles and Peter decided to keep him in Gaba and help him get his education. While there Fred had to work pushing a wheelbarrow of fish every day on the shores of Lake Victoria, just to stay in school.

Fred had received a camera from an elderly lady who sponsored him while he was there so he learned how to take pictures with it. Also, he had worked for a time for an NGO in Uganda, profiling families for them. He was a strong Christian, a member of the church at Gaba, and had been mentored by both Charles and Peter. Besides, he had already contributed a lot to the plan that Charles had put together for Africa New Life. It seemed to Charles that he was a perfect choice.

However, Fred had seen Charles struggle in his early ministry with poverty. He knew how difficult it had been for Charles, and Fred wanted none of that. He had left his home and come to live with Charles in hopes of finishing his education and going to the city to get a good-paying job. Fred wanted to manage things, to be a businessman, to have a comfortable city life. He had great dreams!

But while he was going back and forth to Rwanda for Charles, Fred asked God, "Is this something you want me to do?" During that time, he says he opened the Bible in Exodus to the conversation God has with Moses from the burning bush.

In this Scripture God tells Moses, "I have surely seen the affliction of My people who are in Egypt, and have given heed to their cry, because of their taskmasters, for I am aware of their sufferings." He then tells Moses, "Come now, and I will send you to Pharaoh, so that you may bring My people, the sons of Israel out of Egypt."

Going back and forth, Fred couldn't get that Scripture passage out of his mind. God truly cared for those who suffered. He'd heard the cry of the orphans, the widows, the hurting families in Rwanda. Was Fred part of His plan to help them?

Now here was Charles on the phone, asking him to come and direct the school, and help to oversee the ministry. At this time Fred had a comfortable life, a fruitful ministry, enough money for food, and a good place to stay.

"Let me pray about it," he told Charles.

And he did pray! He also decided to talk to his good friend and mentor, Pastor Peter. Peter told him that he was a valuable asset and had a great future right there in Gaba. "After all," Peter told him, "Rwanda is not stable yet. Why would you want to risk your life? If you go, you need to be very sure that God in the one calling you to work with your brother."

After some more discussion, Peter advised Fred to travel to Rwanda for a month and "spy out the land" just like the Israelites did before they were to cross over the Jordan River into the Promised Land. In that story, only two of the twelve spies came back with a favorable report. The others saw the obstacles and lacked faith in God to accomplish what He had asked them to do. Peter encouraged Fred to trust God to show him if indeed this was the right way to go.

So Fred took a few weeks off and left for Rwanda. He had heard about a conference and decided to go, thinking that focusing on God while he was there would probably help him discern whatever God wanted him to do. As he entered the building where the conference was to be held, he saw a large banner hung over the doorway. It said, "Spy Out the Land." The conference was about having faith in God and trusting Him to do the impossible. It was about believing that God would provide for you if you were involved in work He set before you.

After the conference, Fred found out about another leadership conference. As he walked in he saw that the conference title was the very same: "Spy Out the Land." He left the next morning, went back to Gaba, turned in his resignation and began to make plans to move to Rwanda.

Meanwhile, Florence and Charles were already busy. They bought some benches, some tables, and rented a small house.

Fred soon arrived to help with the school administration, child sponsorship, property purchases, and all of the other details necessary to establish a school.

Specioza, their sister who was living in Kayonza with her parents, became the headmistress of the small school under the leadership of Fred. They hired one teacher. Konsalata brought food from her garden and did whatever she could for the children. On September 17, 2001, New Life Nursery School opened to help orphans and children from poor families get a pre-primary education.

The following year in Portland was very hectic. Charles graduated ahead of Florence with a Master of Arts degree in Ministry Management. He was still flying to England and flying to Rwanda, working on all three continents.

In addition, he was helping establish Africa New Life Ministries as a legitimate organization, selecting a board of directors, finding a sponsor umbrella organization, and coordinating with Fred and the others in Rwanda.

Dr. Robnett made it possible for the ministry to join under the umbrella of Faith in the Family International, since he was a board member.

Serena, as a CPA, helped to set up an accountability system to manage the funds of the fledgling ministry. This arrangement protected the resources for the children, until a Board of Directors was formed and many of the other organizational arrangements could be put into place.

Many of these details were made possible by the hard work and generous hearts of Tony and Serena, now very close friends. Florence was also finishing her degree in Family Ministries and taking care of their three children.

At the same time, they began to work on the ministry, to put into practice the plan. Charles and Florence came back to America with thirty pictures, children Specioza had taken them to see who were photographed by Fred.

Tony and Serena had a large home and invited some friends to presentations they called "Africa Nights." A local restaurant owner offered to cook traditional African meals.

They soon had sponsors for all thirty kids. "We were very happy about that!" says Charles. But it was just the beginning.

Fred sent more batches of photos and they expanded Africa Nights to as many homes as they could.

Charles sought speaking engagements in local churches in Portland and went wherever he could to tell others about the new ministry and to preach the Gospel.

By the time they actually arrived in Kigali they had sponsors for 100 children. Property for the school in Kayonza had already been bought. Miriam and Don Egan from England provided the funds for this initial property. Meanwhile, New Life Family church in England also bought a very large piece of land and funded the first orphanage.

During these fundraising trips Charles met Papa Bill as he is affectionately called by everyone at Africa New Life. His formal name is Colonel William B. Driggers, Jr. and he is retired from twenty-six years of Air Force service, another twenty-five years of successful congressional relations experience, and nine years as President of W. B. Driggers and Associates, a government relations consulting firm. He is now Vice Chairman of the ANLM board and a proud sponsor of seventeen children through ANLM.

Bill says he had a conviction to help the children because of a sponsorship commercial on television. An African mother was holding a little baby while the speaker related that due to a disease in her village, the mother had already lost two children and would lose the one she was holding within several months. Bill says he began thinking about how much he and Susan, his wife, love their two sons. He told me as he was sharing this, "God puts a special love in a mother's heart. I knew she must be suffering a lot of grief. I felt I had to do something."

Fifteen months later in northern Virginia, Charles was visiting Marty Granger, the president of Faith in the Family, and came to speak to Bill's Sunday school class about sponsors for the Rwandan children.

Bill remembers that Charles talked about ANLM and their desire to get up to five hundred child sponsorships. He says that, although it had been over a year, he was still thinking about that lady holding her baby. His heart was pricked once again. This time he prayed: "Father, I'm going to dive in head first, so if it's not what You want, grab me by the heels and yank me back."

Then he told Charles he would sponsor ten children! Bill chuckles as he shares the reaction he got from Charles that day, almost as if he wasn't sure he actually understood him.

Papa Bill can describe each of his seventeen ANLM children in detail: he wants to be a pastor; she likes to run and beats the boys to the ball every time; he will be a lot taller than me; he's quiet but he's always around making sure he hears everything; she's having problems with her eyes; he's a quiet kid and his mother has AIDS; her father is in prison; he has a toothpaste smile. He knows all about them because whenever he goes to Rwanda, he visits each one of them.

To listen to Bill talk about the kids he sponsors through ANLM is to understand the heartbeat of the ministry. As part of their philosophy ANLM encourages sponsors to visit their children; their staff members go out of their way to arrange mission trips, visits to children's homes, and—for groups—Westernized accommodations with plenty of water, beds, and wireless connections.

Bill recalls the first big project he was involved in with Charles in Kayonza. "Let's build a dining hall in Kayonza," Charles said to the board in March 2006. "We estimate we need about $77,000 to do it." The board discussed the project and the funding for it. Bill remembers, "I had just picked up a client and the amount of the tithe would be exactly that amount. My first thought was my Father is telling me something." The Board all agreed they should proceed.

Bill says he learned a lot from this project. One of the first things he learned was that Charles didn't waste time. He says they had a machine to make bricks (concrete blocks) and went right to work. Not long after Grace Chapel in Oregon sent a donation of $50,000. Considering this donation, Charles expanded his vision to include a nice kitchen and a larger hall.

Bill laughingly recalls hearing Charles preach, saying, "Your Bible study isn't finished until you practice it." Bill says when Charles sees God opening a door of ministry, he doesn't hesitate. He moves quickly through the door and then asks, "What does He want us to be doing?"

That December, while on a trip to assist ANLM with accounting procedures, Serena sent out an email saying thirteen things had to be done for the building to become useable. Fifteen minutes later there was an email from Charles saying, "We've already been in the building using it for two months. Africa standards are not the same as American standards." Of course, all of Serena's suggestions were implemented—while the building was in use.

Although the cost of the building kept increasing (from the initial $77,000 to $87,000 to $108,000, to $126,000 and finally to $146,000), the money kept coming in. Because ANLM had not built a building of this size before, there were many unanticipated changes in the plans as the building took shape. And people came to help from all over.

The building, begun in March 2006, was completed in December. It is the largest building in the province and is appropriately named the Life Center. It is the center of nearly all the Academy, Orphanage, and Church activities. The teachers in the province have teachers' conferences there; the church meets there every Sunday; the teachers have a time of devotion there weekly; the children eat there every day of the week; and there are special concerts and summer programs. It is a busy place!

John Africa, headmaster of the Kayonza Africa New Life School, says with considerable pride, "We aren't the biggest school, but we have the biggest building."

Bill ends his description of all this by saying, "You have to watch Charles. Charles had previously mentioned that he wanted a chapel there—shaped like a cross. The architect's drawing had the chapel building appearing almost as large as the Life Center (remember this is the largest building in the whole province). Alan tells me it's an architectural mistake. I'm willing to take all bets that the chapel will be built. With the current growth rate it will certainly be needed. Once Charles starts scheming, big things happen."

He adds, "It's so beautiful to be working with people who are so positive. I get to see my God at work. God brings everything together."

Chapter 12

The Children and Mothers of Kigali

The highest form of worship is the worship of unselfish Christian service. The greatest form of praise is the sound of consecrated feet seeking out the lost and helpless.
—**Billy Graham**, *World Evangelist*

When we finally arrived in Rwanda, Florence and I met scores of children on the streets of Kigali, spent time getting to know them, and then, with Fred's help, began getting sponsorships lined up in Kigali as well as in Kayonza. God has given us grace and favor to work with children. For us, children are the most vulnerable part of society.

I remember being a child refugee and the kind of abuse and beatings I endured, being denied my own rights. I don't want those kinds of things to happen to these children. So, when we go into a community we go to help the children first.

When I look into the eyes of these orphans and other children who are raised in dysfunctional families, I can see that their greatest needs are security and a father figure. The biggest challenge we face in our work is not only to make sure their needs are met, but also to provide a secure environment and a father figure in the absence of their lost fathers and families. The post-genocide Rwanda is a fatherless society. As such it is a very insecure society. In contrast, God designed functional families not only to provide for needs, but to provide security as well. Wars that kill parents and destroy families leave children running for their lives without help and protection.

Through child sponsorship, education, and meeting physical and spiritual needs, we hope to provide the kind of

> loving environment that gives these children back their sense
> of security and hope.

Almost as soon as their feet touched Rwandan soil, Charles and Florence began to work on developing the ministry.

Life was hard when they first arrived, but they had hope. They had saved a small amount of money and borrowed an office chair and a table. Eventually they were able to get beds. Florence carried Isaac on her back as she went to the market and began to get to know the people.

Florence says of that time, "We just kept going. But that's Charles and that's us. To be able to help many lives you have to make sacrifices. Charles is a strong man yet he is very positive. He would be positive in the middle of very hard circumstances— that was very helpful."

Charles, ever mindful of the sacrifices he asked of Florence, found a tiny home he could fix up. He began to add on to it (a wife, three kids and a myriad of future ministry visitors would need space, after all).

Florence remembers: "We saved a lot for our home. We prayed for a home during our honeymoon. We had an old truck in which he carried the sand and bricks so that he could build the new addition. He was a crazy construction man! He would get up at six in the morning and come home well after dark, because he was also building the ministry, making connections, ministering to the street children, working with his new staff, and overseeing construction of the school and orphanage.

"His old car would stall out at the traffic light sometimes but the street kids knew him and would go and push his car to get it off the road. This was how it was with Charles," she finishes with a grin.

UNICEF has been actively involved in Rwanda the past two years. At http://www.unicef.org/infobycountry/rwanda.html are many articles describing the plight of the Rwandan child today. Here are some of the facts presented in those reports:

> (1) Neonatal deaths are still high in Rwanda, at 37 per 1,000 live births, although progress has been made in this area.

(2) One out of every ten Rwandan children continues to die before their fifth birthday, mostly from preventable causes such as pneumonia, malaria, diarrhea, and chronic malnutrition. More than 80 percent of all diseases that affect Rwandan children are waterborne.

(3) In Rwanda, 45 percent of children under five are chronically malnourished or stunted.

(4) Half of Rwanda's citizens are under the age of 18. Most of these children live on less than $1 a day. Many are still recovering from the 1994 genocide and its aftermath.

(5) While overall HIV prevalence remains low (about 3 percent), only half of all children in need of anti-retroviral treatment receive it. Some 250,000 people are estimated to be living with HIV in Rwanda with 22,000 children under the age of 15.

(6) Of the children who enroll in school, half do not complete the primary cycle. Approximately 4 percent of children aged 5 to 14 are working, mostly in domestic service and the informal economy.

(7) Over half of all households are either food-insecure or vulnerable due to fluctuations in global food prices, natural disasters, as well as loss of soil productivity and the steadily shrinking per capita availability of arable land.[1]

While these fact paint a bleak picture, it would not be fair to fail to give credit to the post-genocidal Rwandan government led by Paul Kagame and extending down to the regional and provincial leaders. In cooperation with many outside organizations, they have spearheaded outstanding public works, and developed comprehensive plans to improve the plight of children and women in Rwanda. They are beginning to see a number of positive results.

An article for the *Philadelphia Inquirer* written by Andrew Maykuth, describes the current situation for the children of Rwanda this way:

"Against this unstable backdrop on both sides of the Congo-Rwanda border, children are raising children inside Rwanda in desperate poverty, with unknown consequences for the future of Rwandan society. Forty-six percent of the population is under 15. UNICEF estimates that 300,000 Rwandan children are growing up in families without adults—almost 5 percent of the population, and about 10 percent of all children under 18... No one is quite sure what the long-term effect of so many parentless children will be on such a small and weak nation."[2]

In a nation where neighbor killed neighbor, and relatives were forced to kill their kin, the traditional family structure that is the bedrock of African culture was as much a victim of the genocide as the hundreds of thousands who died. Before the genocide, orphanages were virtually unknown because relatives or communities took in orphans.

"In 15 to 20 years' time, if nothing is done now, there will be another problem," said Nigel Marsh, spokesman for World Vision International, which conducted the study for UNICEF. "We don't know what that will be. There's no precedent for a country having 300,000 people who grow up without parents. It's a tremendous psychosocial problem."[3]

Indeed, these next years will be a great time of stress for the little nation. Refugees are coming back; Tutsis and Hutus are being forced out of Burundi and Tanzania. Now, they are struggling to find a way to survive together again. Murderers and the innocent are being released from prison as well. Some of them still harbor deep hatred.

In addition, when you visit Rwanda, it is not uncommon to find people with mental health problems all around the country due to Post-Traumatic Stress Disorder (PTSD). Some researchers have said that 90 percent of the children in Rwanda remain traumatized by the war of 1994.

Charles discovered that he too suffered from PTSD because of the war experiences he went through as a child. In documenting the needs of the children of Rwanda, he distilled these symptoms from a book he read:

(1) Recurrent distressing dreams of the event.

(2) Recurrent and intrusive distressing recollections of the event (in young children, repetitive play in which themes or aspects of the trauma are expressed).

(3) Sudden acting or feeling as if the traumatic event is recurring (illusions, hallucinations, flashback episodes).

(4) Intense psychological distress at exposure to events that symbolize or resemble an aspect of the traumatic event.

(5) Markedly diminished interest in significant activities (in young children there can be a loss of recently acquired developmental skills such as toilet training or language).

(6) Feelings of detachment or estrangement from others.

(7) Unable to have loving feelings.

(8) Difficulty falling or staying asleep.

(9) Outbursts of anger.

(10) Morbid hatred: obsessions of vengeance and preoccupation with hurting or humiliating the perpetrator, with or without outbursts of anger or rage.[4]

The results of PTSD in various manifestations have been repeatedly witnessed by the teachers and leaders of ANLM. A number of children have parents who have such mental duress that they run away to the streets or bush. Sadly, some never return home.

Such symptoms are not entirely unlike those experienced by many American soldiers returning from Iraq and Afghanistan.

In Rwanda, many children still exhibit depression, are uninterested in life, are very slow to learn, or can express anger unrelated or unconnected to the circumstances around them. They can behave in surprising ways and without provocation. Most of these kids are highly reserved and very touchy. They don't want to mix with other kids. They are unwilling to trust other kids, even those who want to help them.

Perhaps the most disconcerting symptom is morbid hatred, which could manifest itself in future periods of civil unrest. Although great strides have been made toward reconciliation and stability, the 2010 presidential elections did not proceed without violence.

What can be done to help children overcome some of these difficulties in spirit, mind and body? The philosophy for ANLM schools was developed by Charles partly through his direct involvement with students in his early teaching days with Pastor Bunkenya in Gaba, where he worked with student ministries, as well as during his time at seminary.

In the summer of 2001 Charles set forth four principles that guide ANLM teachers to this day:

(1) Parents must be encouraged to work with teachers in the education of their children.

(2) Every child can learn. So, teachers must strive to use all available educational methods to fit each child's individual learning style. Teachers also must keep classroom discussions and communication open in order to provide learning opportunities for every child.

(3) Demonstrated love for each child is the greatest key for inspired learning, and will build a desire to succeed and self-confidence in every student.

(4) Biblical teaching, along with subject mastery, is able to produce literate, hardworking, frugal, and respectful young men and women who can discern between right and wrong objectively.[5]

Rwanda needs a transformation. Only God can do that! On the 2010 anniversary of the end of the 1994 genocide I told my congregation, "Only God can give you the forgiveness you need." God is the changer! He is the forgiver! Rwanda cannot do this without God.

Africa New Life is not just a humanitarian ministry. We are an evangelistic ministry, one that focuses on teaching and preaching the Gospel of the kingdom of God to His people in Rwanda. The ANLM mission statement is transforming lives and communities through proclaiming the Gospel and acts of compassion. This is a two-handed approach, based on Matthew 9:12. Jesus Christ saw the people as hopeless and hungry, dispirited and sick, describing them as sheep without a shepherd.

Throughout the Gospels we see Jesus preaching about the kingdom of God. He is very clear about the kingdom of

God, but He is also feeding the people and healing the sick. This is how I feel God wants us to minister in Rwanda.

In ministry, these are two hands working together, not one hand working at one time and the other working at another time, but two hands actively engaged in the harvest. I believe that the harvest is ready in Rwanda. As I've said before, when the harvest is ready you use both hands concurrently.

My father grew up growing coffee and, when it is ready, you must use both hands and harvest the coffee very quickly. Interestingly, when you pick coffee there are parts of the tree that can be reached with one hand and other parts that can be reached more easily with the other. You also borrow as many hands as you possibly can because the time to harvest can be so short.

So our ministry uses one hand to proclaim the Gospel, to teach and to preach the word of God. The other hand is the hand of compassion. We feed the poor, provide training to widows, house orphans, find sponsorship and provide counseling to the many families who are so damaged by what has happened.

I remind everyone that when you use one hand and don't use the other hand, you are crippled.

Clearly, ANLM doesn't just focus on the children. By developing relationships with kids on the streets of Kigali, Florence and Charles began to meet the widows and poorer women around them as well. Almost 42 percent of the female population of Rwanda is widowed. Many others must head households because their husbands are in jail serving sentences or awaiting trials for their part in the genocide.

AIDS is also a problem, particularly among the street women and the refugees who have returned to Rwanda. Women and their daughters who were either Tutsi or married to Tutsi were raped, many by men infected with AIDS. This was an intentional act of genocide, to degrade the women as much as possible, but also to ensure their death and the death of their offspring.

In addition, thousands of Rwandans fled to United Nations refugee camps to escape the genocide campaigns. These camps became notorious for prostitution and sexual promiscuity, further spreading AIDS among the women and their unborn children.

Florence has always had a dream of helping women. Growing up in a poor village, Florence had seen many women digging in the dirt with kids on their backs, doing hard work with no chance of getting an education or developing a trade. So she wrote in the plan for Africa New Life that she would love to see women given a chance to acquire an education or a real skill so that they wouldn't always have to labor so hard.

Now, Florence was back in Rwanda. What could she do? She had two sewing machines, so she began a sewing ministry. She taught women to sew five days a week and also discipled them. She began with a six-month training program, but decided to expand it.

The women also needed to know about parenting, building healthy families, nutrition, and hygiene. There are some requirements for participation: you must be a female at least 18 years of age with accommodations, you must be able to study, and you must be truly interested. The program, however, is not limited to church members.

Florence says, "There are many women in this program who learn to sew or to braid hair as a trade. In the end, women need to feel like women again." They are women who have no other means of survival.

Some are genocide survivors who were not able to go to school. Some are single mothers who never had an opportunity to go to school or were forced by their families to labor in the fields as early as third grade. Some are women who are HIV positive or street women whose families sent them away because they could no longer feed them. And, some have husbands who are drug addicts.

These women work in a small room filled with sewing machines, learning to custom fit patterns, cut, and sew, and developing the patience and craft of a seamstress. They also receive counseling from Florence and enjoy times of worship together.

Florence often shares some of her favorite verses from the Bible. She quotes Psalms 139:14, "I am fearfully and wonderfully made." Then she tells the women, "You are special.

Don't steal and don't mess up your life. Your heart has to know this—you are so special to God! You must know this here in your heart," she says and pats her chest. She then goes on to tell them from Genesis 1:26 that they were created in God's image. "This too makes you special," she tells them.

In Kigali, Africa New Life Ministries—under Florence's compassionate and loving guidance—is making a difference among the women. Hundreds of women and children are being transformed by the love of God and by the love of hundreds of Christians from around the globe who pray, give, or serve in partnership with ANLM.

One of the women who graduated from the program in 2009 has six orphans living with her. Three of them have AIDS and she does, too. However she says that since she received Jesus Christ, there has been peace in her heart. She says God always provides enough for her and the children—not a lot, but enough.

Another woman in the sewing program was one of the children left behind after the genocide and has lived with various families, moving from one position of servitude to another.

Now with ANLM's help, she is getting her education so, even though her current family isn't very good to her, she can look forward to a better life.

And that's what ANLM wants for these women—a better life. It costs about $2,000 American dollars to start a cooperative of ten women sewing together. With that money they can purchase enough cloth and thread and a sewing machine to begin a cottage business. ANLM hopes to find sponsors for these women who would be willing to send $60 a year.

Street children also find hope and a better future because of ANLM sponsors. One of the earlier kids to find his way off the street and into life as a Christian is Enric Sifa.

Enric Sifa laughs a lot. He's short, really cute, and usually sports a hat. When he's not studying, Enric goes on music concert tours raising funds for Africa New Life Ministries. In his early twenties he is concerned with his first year in college in the United States. He has some years to make up.

You see, he is also a young man who lost part of his family, including his parents, in the 1994 Rwandan genocide.

At nine years old Enric was out on his own, living on the street in Kigali, Rwanda.

He says, "I would get up and go and shoot marbles. We would do that for hours. If I won, I would go and buy food and then go to the movies. You see, each movie lasted a few hours and the days go by slow when you are out on the street. So you could see three movies and then that was six hours gone and the day would be shorter."

He adds, "If I didn't win at marbles, I would go out looking for luggage to carry. People would pay you a little bit and then you could eat."

One Saturday night Enric went to one of the bars nearby. He loved music and had heard that a famous musician would be playing. But that night he didn't get a chance to hear any music. Instead, he was severely beaten for attempting to get in; street kids are often targets for bullying.

After being beaten up Enric went to sleep on the street and heard a voice talking to him. "You don't need to go to bars and clubs to find joy," the voice said. "There is something better for you."

Enric says: "I didn't know it was the voice of God, but for sure it was because it was so peaceful. Next day while I was just walking in town, I heard music in a building. I didn't know it was church, but I was desperate for music. I went to check it out and when I entered people were dancing, smiling, singing, and full of joy. The music was free and no one was there to beat me up. After that I kept going back, and as the days went on God revealed his truth to me and I fell in love with Jesus."

At that church Enric found acceptance and warmth. More importantly, he was sponsored and now had a new home and "family."

One of Enric's favorite things growing up was receiving letters from his American sponsor. These letters proved to him that somebody cared about him, that somebody knew his name, and that gave him the confidence to pursue his dream of becoming a musician.

In fact, at church Enric's musical abilities were actively encouraged. Soon he was teaching songs to the younger children.

Enric was fifteen years old when he was given his first guitar. He remembers that day very well.

Several years later, the Rwandan government sponsored a national contest for the best song about AIDS. Enric entered a song he wrote and won. Suddenly he was a celebrity on the order of "American Idol" or "America's Got Talent."

Even today if you get into a taxi in Rwanda, you'll probably hear Enric's songs on the radio or CD player. Whenever Enric travels back to Africa, especially to Rwanda, he often has to travel with someone else; girls flock to his concerts and scream his name. He's a true star!

With much levity, Enric hams it up around a table with Charles, Fred, and Alan Hotchkiss. During the conversation, fatherly advice and teasing are dished out by all three men. Enric is still part of the African New Life family.

Enric is quick to tell everyone that he is a Christian. He shares his faith and is bold about what he believes. His musical style, he says, is soul pop. His favorite artists include Seal and John Regent. Now he plays simply as Enric and has his own Christian band here in the U.S.

If he hadn't received one of ANLM's child sponsorships, Enric says he would be dead or in serious trouble by now. Instead, he looks forward to furthering his education and he continues to sing for God's glory.

Changing lives through compassion and the Good News of Jesus Christ—that's what ANLM is all about! These are just a few examples of the thousands of lives already changed by sponsors who care.

**While we can't change the whole world,
we can change the world for one!**

Chapter 13

The Dream Center

"Have faith in God. Truly I say to you, whoever says to this mountain, 'Be taken up and cast into the sea,' and does not doubt in his heart, but believes that what he says is going to happen, it shall be granted him. Therefore I say to you, all things for which you pray and ask, believe that you have received them, and they shall be granted you."
—Jesus (Matthew 11:22-24)

Charles and Florence had just arrived back in Rwanda. It was November 2003 and the new ANLM Board of Directors had flown in to help the ministry get under way. Marvin Egglestone, board chairman, Rob Bauer, Tony Morones, and Charles were driving through the national park when they decided to start a church.

"Why not?" Charles asked. "Let's go start it; I have my family and we have a lot of street children around us."

They found a small property near the center of Kigali, the capitol of Rwanda, and the location of many of the street children Florence and Charles had targeted for ministry.

Charles called his friend, Pastor Eliseé, who put up a sign announcing the new church. The property had no building, but Marvin gave them $6,000. With that they put up a wood structure and tin roof and held their first church service the very next Sunday.

They fasted and prayed for forty days as soon as the church began. Charles says, "We were so happy about the church, about this new arm of the Gospel in Rwanda, and just to be doing what we had wanted to do for so many years. Since we knew that Jesus fasted for forty days in spiritual preparation for his ministry, we decided to do the same thing. I believe this helped us face the coming challenges."

As soon as they had their little church going, and fifty people were coming every Sunday, the owner of the property decided to sell the land. He gave them fifteen days to vacate the property. It was a stunning blow.

I didn't know where to go. I was just beginning and the evil one was cutting it off. So we prayed that God would help us.

The night after we were told to leave the property, a young lady who helped us with the children came and told us about a dream she had.

She dreamed that she was in a church, our church, and that the building had green glass and a floor covered with tiles. That was very interesting, especially since we didn't have any money or any property on which to build such a nice church. It didn't connect. We were just looking for a church to survive.

Norman Desire, a local evangelist, came to me and said, "Charles, there's a new building they are constructing by your church. Do you want to go there and see it and try to rent it?" That's the place I expected least to get—it was a beautiful place. The cost of rent was over $1,000. I talked to the ANLM Board of Directors in the U.S. and a number of our friends and somehow God provided the money.

While we were there looking over the building, a young wiry white guy shows up wanting to meet us. John Crocker, who had been a missionary in Africa for a number of years, happens to be from Huntsville, Alabama, and was visiting Rwanda to see if his church could help with missions work there. He has since become one of our U.S. partners.

The church moved on a Sunday. Nobody knew they were moving until they showed up. I preached on moving by faith into the Promised Land. Then I had everyone pick up their chair and follow me into the new little jewel of a church. We crossed the Red Sea—crossing over from Egypt to the Promised Land.

It was a beautiful place, but very small. The church could grow to only about 200. That would not do for the God-sized plan I had developed at Multnomah, but it was actually a blessing. We had been blown by a big wind on the sea and this was a nice place to rest for a bit.

At that point the overall ANLM ministry in Kigali was fragmented. There was a house for the family center, a building for Sunday worship, and a center for the street children (a feeding station)—all in different places.

This made communication and management difficult. There was no synergy and every ministry director was on their own little island, so to speak.

Soon Charles began to feel his team was beginning to come apart, and their unity was under attack by the "old dragon." Then he found a huge old warehouse. Under that one roof he could bring all of the team members together and all of the ministries —including a future training center.

Charles found himself wandering over to that building a few times thinking, *What we could do with this kind of place!* But the owners of the building wanted half a million dollars. How could his fledgling ministry raise that kind of money when they could barely pay $1,000 a month to rent their current church building?

Then again, Charles had seen God motivate people to send him to England, seen God remove the witches in Gaba, seen God bring this team of dedicated teachers and leaders together over the years, and seen God provide for his needs over and over again in order to advance the kingdom of Christ.

So Charles took a number of church members over to the old warehouse. Then he took a couple of ministry teams there. Everyone was afraid of the price; the price was enormous. Everyone felt it was completely out of the range. "You are not realistic," they chided.

"In my heart, though, I felt God was about to do something," remembers Charles. "When God gives you a dream, He doesn't show you, most of the time, how He's going to make it happen."

Charles couldn't shake the feeling that God wanted them to buy the old warehouse. At this time, Dave, Tony and Serena in Portland were getting ready to have a banquet. This would become an annual by-invitation-only event to raise money and ministry awareness.

Just before Charles was to leave for the United States to attend the banquet, he had a visit from a pilot from Grace Chapel, Marlin Dumler, who had flown Rick Warren to Rwanda. He sought out Charles because he was sponsoring a child through ANLM. Charles showed him their current church and then the "dream" building. After Charles shared his vision, Marlin told him to look him up when he got to the U.S. because he wanted him to meet his boss.

This connection would prove to be beneficial, resulting in several substantial donations, the first one making the Dream Center a reality! At the banquet in Portland, they raised an additional $250,000 for what they began to call the Dream Center. There was a commitment from their friends in Huntsville, headed up by John Crocker, as well. Yet, it wasn't fast enough. Within days Charles received word from home that someone else had bought the old warehouse.

Charles remembers the struggle this created within him. The building was gone and so was his dream. He felt discouraged, defeated, and ashamed. In his discouragement, Charles said to God, "Do you want us to do this?"

It was a dark time.

Charles explains: "If you are a visionary and you don't have proof [he holds out his hands, palms up, empty] that means that you led your people to the wrong destination."

More bad news surfaced soon: someone with more money wanted to lease the building where they were currently having church. So, the owners were asking them to leave.

"How could I be so wrong," thought Charles. "Didn't God want us to raise this money? Now we have all of this money and nothing to buy with it and nowhere to have church."

> My favorite Bible chapter is Matthew 6, verses 25 and on. It is beautiful and during this time my wife suggested I read it. I dwelt there for a while. *"Don't be anxious for your life, you will never be as smart or as well-dressed as the lilies of the valley."* Now that's beautiful, isn't it?
>
> I believe in the providence of God. If we need something and we call upon Him, He will provide it. This passage sets out a number of conditions, but it is also comforting. If you have

life, He will give you the food you need; if you have a body, He will give you the clothing you need.

So, *don't be anxious.* Instead, just relax. Reflect upon the past and remember what God has done. Where you are today is the tomorrow you worried about yesterday.

"Are you not worth much more than they are—the sparrows and the lilies?" I have value before Him. You can't change anything, why are you worked up? Relax! You can't change anything by being worried. Observe! Why are you anxious? *The lilies don't toil or spin—even Solomon in his glory didn't have clothes as beautiful as these flowers.*

"You men of little faith," says Jesus. He issues a challenge to us right here. We really have such little faith. *"Don't look for the things the Gentiles seek; your Father knows what you need."* God is not against providing for us. He's not against us having things, but that shouldn't be your focus. Instead, God says, *"Your focus should be My kingdom. All these things will be added unto you,* whether here in heaven or there on earth."

This passage got me through a lot of difficult days.

The Lord did have something different and better for them than what Charles and his friends had already seen. Soon they found out about another piece of land. There was nothing already built on it except a few smaller buildings. It was a larger property, and open land, which were both difficult to find in the crowded city. Better yet, it was in the heart of the area where the street kids and the poor lived. What's more, a new highway was scheduled to be built right next to it.

Charles tells of standing on the dirt where Africa New Life Dream Center is now and seeing the buildings in his mind. He saw a beautiful worship center, offices for the ANLM staff, a building so the street boys could learn carpentry, a family center where women could come and receive sewing and Bible study training while their kids were being taken care of by sitters, and a brand-new Bible college.

Nothing ever gets built unless someone envisions it first. "Without faith it is impossible to please God," it says in

Hebrews 11. Faith begins by envisioning the impossible. This is a God-sized dream because we know we cannot achieve it.

The Great Commission is the only foundation for a dream that will last. All other dreams, climbing up some ladder of success in any area, will come to nothing because the ladder is leaning on a broken wall. Sooner or later it's going to come crashing down.

But God's dreams always come with the power to complete them.

This doesn't mean seeing a "God-sized" dream completed is easy, though!

Charles, Pastor Eliseé and many others went to work. At the time, the church only had about 200 to 300 people, but they raised $40,000. Pastor Emma was the general contractor on the project.

Everyone was giving. Some people gave one or two months of their salary in a year. I remember one woman brought her jewelry. "This is what I have, Pastor; sell it all." Another woman came to me and said, "I got a new job that doubled my salary." Everyone gave sacrificially toward the Dream Center project. That building was born in seven months.

For me, though, the birthing of this project was a time of personal trial. The devil is a bad devil. Everything seemed to be coming together for the Dream Center when, toward the conclusion of the project, I ended up with a hernia. This resulted in a stint in the hospital with an operation that didn't go well, trapping some of my nerves.

That was a dark time for me. I struggled for about seven months. I had a hard time walking, so I ran meetings flat on my back from home on the phone. One builder fell from the building and terribly injured himself; Florence didn't want to tell me. Then, I had to go back to the hospital, this time with malaria. The day I got home, I told them to take me to the Dream Center. I had to see it.

As you enter the worship center, you see domed ceilings with acoustical tiling, creamy beige walls, graduated seating, and multi-level staging covered in creamy white tiles, which contrast with the dark red soil of Rwanda outside.

This is a pearl of a building, a place of purity, a place of hope, and a place of love, built for the poor in their own neighborhood. This is a building for weddings, joyful praise and worship, christenings of new life, baptisms celebrating lives born again into the most important of Kingdoms, God's kingdom, and healing for wounded hearts and hurting widows.

At the very first community celebration after the building was complete, the young adult choir hosted another young adult choir and a traditional African dance troupe. It was a joyful celebration and many church members attended, some community dignitaries, even a group of men and women from the U.S. While the evening progressed, children crept into the Dream Center and sat down.

The children came in little clumps, mostly boys, some about nine years old carrying four-year-olds, many with matted hair, runny noses, sores, dirty feet, ragged clothes, obviously children from the streets, mingling with all of the others and enjoying the concert. As they entered, they found seats, some snuggling next to adults in attendance who opened their arms to them. They were at home here in this place. And it was clear that this was as much their place as anyone else who was there that night.

The Dream Center is a work in progress. For now small buildings on the premises are used as work centers and classrooms. There is a ministry to the children of the streets, so dear to the heart of Charles and Florence, which provides food, clothing, and bathing soap and water twice a week. Sponsorships provide schooling for these children.

In addition, those who are too old for school are offered apprenticeships in the ANLM carpentry shop, a small dirt floored area. Another small building houses the family center, which holds the beauty shop and sewing center as well as a small store where widows and young women with no means of support can come and learn to sew. The heartbeat of this ministry is Florence and it is her desire to see every woman learn about Jesus Christ, how to manage their households, how to raise their children, as well as how to sew. Sponsors can provide funds to help these women launch their home businesses once they complete their training.

Christian workers receive training at this center since there is no theological training available in Rwanda. Plans call for a vocational center and additional classrooms for ministerial training, as well as improved facilities for the street children and the widows.

The day the small church moved into the new Dream Center, Charles preached a sermon he titled, Daring to Dream the Dream of God. In the sermon he told about many great men and women who came from humble beginnings and obscure backgrounds, many from the streets, who had very little, yet who are used by God to impact their generation for Jesus Christ.

He mentioned Dwight L. Moody, a shoemaker, who became one of the greatest evangelists and promoters of education America has ever known. He spoke at length about David, the average looking shepherd boy who was used by God to establish the foundation of the prophetic, divine, and eternal Kingdom of His Son, Jesus Christ.

He discussed how Nehemiah, a simple servant as a cup-bearer in the house of a king, was used to rebuild the walls of Jerusalem in fifty-two days, providing security to the children of Israel once again.

He told of Martin Luther King, Jr., who gave his considerable talents, great leadership, and ultimately his life to bring true dignity and freedom to the black population of America during the Civil Rights movement of the 1960s.

He mentioned Joseph, who as a boy is despised by his brothers and thrown into slavery, later suffers unjustly in prison, and yet becomes the salvation of his own people during one of the great famines in the Middle East.

And then there is Moses, a survivor of genocide under the tyrannical Egyptian rule of the time, who led his people out to safety as God commanded him.

And also he mentioned Mother Theresa, a small insignificant woman, and her great work in India among the poor; and Paul Kagame, a poor refugee, who now is transforming Rwanda into a new nation without ethnic divisions.

What is the common thread for these men and women who shake their generations? Charles puts it this way:

> People wonder why some achieve great strides, remarkable breakthroughs, and fundamentally impact their generation while others are satisfied to live a life of mediocrity. Dare to dream the dream of God!
>
> There is no hidden formula or unknown secret of success; there is no such a thing as predetermined destiny or perfectly favorable conditions. Success doesn't necessarily take after family backgrounds or educational dispositions. God is a dream-giving God!
>
> Greatness and success are the works of a dream realized. Everyone can and must have a dream. Follow the unfolding of your dream; keep the pursuit of the dream, have the passion of the dream; you will attain the triumph of your God-given dream.
>
> No wonder David said in Psalm 37:4ff: "Delight yourself in the Lord and He will give you the desires of your heart. Commit your way to the Lord; trust in Him and He will do this: He will make your righteousness shine like the dawn, the justice of your cause like the noonday sun. Be still before the Lord and wait patiently for Him; do not fret..."

Chapter 14

Kageyo

Is this not the fast which I choose, to loosen the bonds of wickedness, to undo the bands of the yoke, and to let the oppressed go free, and break every yoke? Is it not to divide your bread with the hungry, and bring the homeless poor into the house; when you see the naked, to cover him; and not to hide yourself from your own flesh? Then your light will break out like the dawn, and your recovery will speedily spring forth; and your righteousness will go before you; the glory of the Lord will be your rear guard. Then you will call and the Lord will answer; you will cry, and He will say, "Here I am."
—Isaiah 58:6-8

In a sermon at the end of the Remembrance of Genocide Week on Sunday, April 22, 2006, Charles chose to focus on God's way of healing people. Many Rwandans are still very troubled by their terrible memories of the genocide.

> To overcome fear, you must fill your heart with love. You have a life to live. Grieve and move on. Focus your eyes on Jesus Christ to become strong. Medicine for fear is passion for Jesus Christ! God specializes in new beginnings. Believe on Him and expect a new life. To retreat into resentment only hurts you. Don't rehearse pain. Let it go. I believe God is going to use each of you in big ways.

It is this determination, this style of kingdom living, that inspires his staff and continues to bring healing, help and hope to untold thousands of Rwandans.

Already, Charles and his team are working in another area of Rwanda. Local officials noticed the work of ANLM in Kayonza

119

and the transformation that occurred in that community over seven years. The children in Kayonza became healthy and well fed. Orphanages were built and the school is now ranked fifth best in all of Rwanda.

With Kayonza as a model, government officials have asked ANLM to help with a desperate situation in Kageyo. This is a remarkable plea since no church has ever before been asked to aid in public education in Rwanda.

Kageyo is tucked into the southeast corner of Rwanda on the border of a national wildlife refuge. During the Rwandan genocides in 1959 and 1994, thousands of people fled the country and settled in neighboring countries, including Tanzania. They started new lives: built homes, got jobs, and purchased land and livestock.

In 2006 and 2007, Tanzania caused an international outcry when it forcibly returned thousands of Rwandan and Burundian refugees and asylum seekers to their native countries.[1] Many of these refugees found themselves headed to Kageyo. Given one day to pack whatever they could carry, the new lives these refugees had worked so hard to establish vanished overnight.

Because of a shortage of land, the Rwandan government struggled to find a place for these refugees to resettle. In many cases the families had been outside Rwanda for two generations, so their land had been parceled out to others years ago. To meet their pressing needs, the government built small homes for the refugees in Kageyo on land within a national park.

The land in Kageyo is not fertile and the arid climate makes sustainable farming very difficult. Kageyo is so remote that its people are struggling to survive; trade and commerce are very difficult. Most of the men have left the area to go and find work, and some never return, leaving women and children without hope of survival.

As you drive up to Kageyo, you see rows of houses built by the government that are fairly good by African standards. What you don't see is much else. Within these houses desperation makes itself at home. The government lacks funding to help these poorest of the poor.

More than 450 families, and more than 1,000 people, have only one low-lying pond to meet all their water needs. Because of the proximity to the wildlife reserve, this pond is often visited by water buffalo, impala, and hippos. The hippos in particular are very dangerous and do not like sharing their watering place. The real cause for concern, however, is that this pond is a source of much sickness for the children of Kageyo. Many of them have suffered from diarrhea due to the polluted water.

According to the Center for Disease Control, two million deaths occur worldwide each year from waterborne illnesses or parasitic infestations, mostly among children under five years of age. And, according to the World Health Organization statistics for Rwanda, some 22 percent of the children under five die from diarrhea each year, the second highest cause of death in the nation (pneumonia being the first).[2] Waterborne bacterial infections may account for as many as half of these episodes and deaths. Many deaths among infants and young children are due to dehydration, malnutrition, or other complications of waterborne bacterial infections.

Another major concern in Kageyo is food scarcity. The arid climate makes sustainable farming difficult. With the wild animal population so close to the village, what crops the community is able to grow often become free food for the animals. Or they shrivel in the bright sun because there is no system of safe irrigation for the crops.

> Kageyo needs a transformation. This transformation will come as we bring faith in Jesus Christ to them. Kageyo needs a hand of compassion as well. The village needs food, clean water, and basic education. We have all the government support to be able to transform Kageyo. God has opened up a door. We don't know how long this door will be open. So, it's now in our hands to get things to happen very quickly in Kageyo to transform that community.
>
> Africa New Life Ministries has already begun to mobilize its volunteers and marshaled its funding efforts to begin buildings to house school teachers, to implement a feeding program, and to begin strategies for sustainable crop production, water sanitation, and medical support.

What does all this mean to those in Kageyo? Hope—hope that leads to community transformation.

One of the many refugees of Kageyo reports: "The journey from Tanzania was very hard. Many, many young ladies of my age passed away. Many other ladies had miscarriages. We came from Tanzania with nothing and my husband soon left to find work. I have not seen him in over a year now. It is just me and my four children."

"Within two or three days of arriving in Kageyo, Africa New Life was helping. My children were some of the first children sponsored. What can I say? Some things words cannot explain. My children are going to school because of Africa New Life. We have been fed nearly every day because of Africa New Life."

"One morning I woke up and went to hear a man speak. He opened the Bible and was talking about a man named Job. When I heard about what he had lost and what he went through, it was no different than what we are going through. That very day, I gave my life to Jesus Christ!"

What will happen in Kageyo over the next three or four years? Will these people be able to build a sustainable, healthy community? That certainly remains to be seen but, with the help of Africa New Life Ministries, there will be a good future.

Chapter 15

The Dream Continues

Be diligent to present yourself approved to God
as a workman who does not need to be ashamed,
accurately handling the word of truth.
—2 Timothy 2:15

Now to Him who is able to do exceeding abundantly beyond all
that we ask or think, according to the power that works within
us, to Him be the glory in the church and in Christ Jesus.
—Ephesians 3:20

In Kigali, when you visit the genocide memorial, you will see signs that say "Never Again!" These signs point to the past; things that have happened and crushed the people, their hearts broken and their dreams turned to dust.

But then you must say, "What next?"

The Kigali Dream Center, the orphanages and school in Kayonza, the new school we are establishing in Kageyo—all point to the future, to hope, and to Jesus Christ.

We are actively preparing for the rebirth of Rwanda, for something new to be born out that pain, out of that dust. Only God can rebuild this nation. You cannot heal a nation without God; He is the great healer! We have a God who never fails, the all-knowing God, the God who hasn't forsaken us!

When the true Gospel is preached, it creates true compassion. The Gospel of our Lord Jesus Christ is full of compassion and His public ministry here on earth was full of compassionate acts.

So, besides working to educate and provide safe, secure environments for the children of Rwanda, we have focused on the need for solid biblical and theological education. I am deeply concerned about the needs of the masses who are without Jesus Christ in so many cities and villages across Africa and among the unevangelized peoples of other lands.

To secure the future and stability of Rwanda and to reach across Africa and around the world, it will take a team of called, anointed, and well-equipped young leaders. African Christians are spiritually motivated and I believe they are being raised up by God in this hour of Christian history to be open to God's working and moving. But we are a well motivated army without the necessary training or equipment!

So, the church needs to be equipping young people in this generation with essential knowledge of God's Word and with practical skills necessary to become powerful witnesses in our mission fields.

In Rwanda today there is the lack of universities designed expressly for training ministers. As a result, the leaders of our churches lack professionalism in defining their ministries and developing their church culture to cope with current secular trends. This allows worldly ideas to creep into the church.

A pastor must be able to define church government and maintain standards in church leadership roles. Theological education will provide sound theological standing, appropriate spiritual vitality, and dynamic evangelistic vision.

To accomplish this goal, however, Africa New Life Ministries must build a training center, equip it, and then be able to give poorer pastors the opportunity to attend without jeopardizing their family and church ministries. How to do this? They have decided to adopt a flexible model, where pastors can attend for a few weeks at a time and be trained by missionary pastors willing to come and serve them.

Already, Charles and his staff have had teams come from the United States to provide conferences and special Bible seminars on leadership, counseling, different books of the Bible, and so on. The planned Bible college training, though, will involve a set curriculum and a planned progression so that each pastor who participates receives a quality education. As he speaks of the Bible College, Charles's passion for excellence, and his desire to share the Gospel message throughout the world, overflow.

Today's world population needs more well trained Gospel heralds. The task of this training calls for commitment to evangelical Bible training now, in Africa, much more than it had been in years past on other continents of the world. We cannot afford to strive for less than the best quality of preparation to the glory of God, our Father.

Africa needs training centers that will not yield to rationalistic or cultural forces. We need centers that will empower the revival movement in Africa—so that it won't wither, especially in view of current attacks of aggressive Islam in North Africa, in the Middle East, in South-East Asia, and in Western Europe.

We visualize a Bible college education that enhances and benefits all, in the name of Jesus Christ and for His honor.

As Africa New Life faces the next few years, there will no doubt be many more challenges ahead. But those involved in Africa New Life, both volunteers and staff, lay leaders and clergy, students and teachers, sense that God is not finished yet!

As Pastor Charles shares his thoughts on his wife's favorite verse, Ephesians 3:20, we are all challenged to dream God-sized dreams, noble dreams that require more than we think and that will take us farther than we anticipate.

Ephesians 3:20 is a packed verse. It begins, "Now to Him who is able...." This gives God a high place! Our God is able because He is all-powerful and all-knowing, omniscient and omnipotent! And He is able to do exceeding abundantly beyond all that we ask or think. I am not sure about the grammatical correctness of this "exceeding abundantly beyond" but it is a good description.

You know, if God had an office, his shingle would say: A Specialist in Impossibilities! When the doctors fail, when your finances fail, when even the government fails, God is constant. We need to put our faith in God. Systems are man-made and they are broken. Only God is unbroken.

Take some time and try to out-imagine God, and then imagine a little more, and then imagine some more, stretching your imagination to its fullest! God then says to you, "I can still beat you! Did you think you asked me for big things?" Faith pleases God and it begins by dreaming and visualizing the invisible. Great things start from small things.

When Florence and I started Africa New Life Ministries, we thought we were asking God for something big, but God has given us something much bigger!

Of course, there's more in this verse: *"...according to the power that works within us, to Him be the glory in the church and in Christ Jesus."*

As members of the Church, you and I have power in Christ! If you are focusing on doing everything to bring glory to God, he will give you a God-sized dream. Everybody needs a dream because if you stop dreaming, you die.

There are five types of people:

(1) Those who have no dreams and exist from day to day just to meet their own small needs. They usually live a life of regret.

(2) Those who have a small dream—get an education, get married, have a job, raise one or two kids, have a big house, send the children to college, then retire and travel across the country in a big van. God wants something more than that from us. He wants us to have a dream that is not about self. Instead, He wants us to dream about sharing the Good News with others. God wants us to dream The Great Commission!

(3) Those who have a wrong dream. There is something they want to achieve and they work very hard at it. Then when they climb the ladder of success in sports or business, they find the ladder is leaning on a broken wall and they come crashing down. It is easy to be a hero today and a zero tomorrow. This world is full of broken things. I don't want to be famous. It is a crumbling wall. Only Jesus is famous and He will be famous forever!

(4) Those who have a vague dream. They do not know what they are supposed to do. They just need to come to Jesus to find their true calling.

(5) Those who have a noble dream; this is a dream that comes from God! Open your mind and ask God to

wake up that dream by His Spirit. Spend significant time with God. Really pray and seek God. We don't spend enough time in His Presence.

Also, be sure to find out what you love to do best and do it for Jesus. The dream God gives you must be more precious than your own comfort. Don't let the challenge of a dream keep you from pursuing it. Don't let criticism keep you from doing it —no one is always happy; you cannot please everybody.

Pursue your dream in the face of obstacles and don't run away. Face your fears. Remember, they are mere shadows cast by Satan to frighten you.

The ANLM directors and staff in Africa and America want everyone to know that they cannot achieve their dreams unless the people of God help them.

There are very few natural resources available in Rwanda and the current government, though making important strides, is still struggling with the major task of building infrastructure for a much overcrowded country. Water is still an ongoing problem as is electricity. Sanitation has yet to be addressed at a national scale although many plans are being developed.

There is always a measure of political struggle as one soon learns from studying African history. The nation is still rife with witchcraft and spiritual suffering. Many people are still searching for reconciliation, forgiveness, and faith.

Why should anyone be confident in a helping the people of a nation like this? Only because God is working in Rwanda!

God is the one in charge of Africa New Life Ministries. And from start to finish, He is doing all of the shaking!

Let's Connect!

Thank you so much for reading this book. Now, we would love to hear from you!

You can contact Charles and Florence, learn more about one of ANLM's women's ministries, and inquire about sponsoring a needy Rwandan child. It takes just a few minutes.

Here's how…

Our mailing address:
Africa New Life Ministries International
P.O. Box 909, Portland Oregon 97207

Our website:
africanewlife.org

Our e-mail address:
book@africanewlife.org

Our phone number:
(503) 906-1590

After contacting us, please don't put this book away. Instead, please invite a small group of friends to go through it with you. You'll find a six-week study guide on pages 137-151. Ask God to use the experience to greatly enrich your life and the lives of your loved ones and friends.

About the Co-Author

Susan W. Lester has a B.S. in English Education and an M.B.A. She has always had a passion for writing and for discipleship, having led more than 40 different groups at last count.

As an empty nester, Susan decided to fulfill a lifelong dream to go on a mission trip with her church to a foreign country. That country was Rwanda, where in 2008 she saw the work of Africa New Life Ministries staff and volunteers first-hand. Less than a year later Susan retired from a staff position at Whitesburg Baptist Church to pursue a full-time writing ministry.

On her way to write her last official article for the newspaper she managed for WBC, she prayed about the children in Rwanda and Africa New Life Ministries (ANLM). With two kids in college, she complained to God that she would have no money to sponsor a Rwandan child now that she wasn't working. So, she asked God to bless the article and to use it to influence someone else to make a dream come true for one of the kids in Rwanda— maybe for several.

Less than two hours later Susan was asked to consider working with Charles, Florence, and others to write this book. It was such an obvious answer to prayer she immediately said yes. So, this is her first book and the fulfillment of another one of her lifelong dreams—to write a book that will make a difference!

Susan lives in Huntsville, Alabama, "the Silicon Valley of the South." She is a very blessed wife to Greg and a very fortunate mother to two children, Lindsey and Michael. You can reach her at susanlester.nobledream@gmail.com. Currently she is editing a few books for some friends, finishing several projects of her own, and looking for God's next assignment to write for the Kingdom—her noble dream!

Notes

Unless otherwise noted, all URLs listed below were accessed as recently as September 3, 2011.

Chapter 1

1. Immaculee Ilibagiza with Steve Erwin, *Left to Tell: Discovering God Amidst the Rwandan Holocaust* (Hay House Inc., 2006), 17.
2. Ugandan Bush War, URL: http://en.wikipedia.org/wiki/Ugandan_Bush_War
3. S.1067 The Lord's Resistance Army Disarmament and Northern Uganda Recovery Act of 2009, Bill 5 of 5, 111th Congress (2009-2010), URL: http://thomas.loc.gov/cgi-bin/query/z?c111:S.1067.ENR:

Additional Sources for History of the Rwandan Genocide:

A. Tracy Kidder, *Strength in What Remains: A Journey of Remembrance and Forgiveness* (Random House, 2009).
B. Stephen Kinzer, *A Thousand Hills: Rwanda's Rebirth and the Man Who Dreamed It* (John Wiley & Sons, Inc., Hoboken, New Jersey, 2008).
C. Kigali Memorial Center Displays, an educational facility which commemorates and documents the genocide in Rwanda as well as provides information on other genocides.

Additional Sources for History of the Luweero War:

A. Alistair Boddy-Evans, Biography, Idi Amin Dada: Despotic president of Uganda in the 1970s, URL: http://africanhistory.about.com/od/biography/a/bio_amin.htm

   B. Idi Amin, URL: http://en.wikipedia.org/wiki/ Idi_Amin

Additional Sources for the U.S. response to the LRA and Child Soldiering in Northern Uganda:

   A. Resolve Uganda: History of the Conflict, URL: http://www.theresolve.org/history
   B. The Christmas Massacres: LRA attacks on Civilians in Northern Congo (Human Rights Watch, February 2009), URL: http://www.hrw.org/sites/default/files/ reports/drc0209web_0.pdf
   C. End Child Soldier Use, World Vision, URL: http://www.worldvision.org/content.nsf/learn/globali ssues-child-soldiers
   D. Charles London, *One Day the Soldiers Came* (Harper Collins Publishers, New York, 2007).

Chapter 4

   1. Dan Bortolotti, *Hope in Hell: Inside the World of Doctors Without Borders* (Firefly Books, 2006), 163. For additional information about malaria, see also http://www.cdc.gov/malaria/about/distribution.html

Chapter 5

   1. Dr. Jack Partain, "Christians and Their Ancestors: A Dilemma of African Theology," paragraph 7, URL: http://www.religion-online.org/showarticle.asp?title =1078 (this article first appeared in the *Christian Century,* November 26, 1986).
   2. Gaba Community Church: Our History, URL: http:// www.gabachurch.org (About Us tab, Our History link).

Chapter 6

   1. "Social Repercussions of The Troubles," URL: http://en. wikipedia.org/wiki/The_Troubles#Social_repercussions For additional information, see: Ann Marie Imbornoni,

Borgna Brunner, and Beth Rowen, "The Northern Irish Conflict: A Chronology—A history of the conflict and the slow progress towards peace," URL: http://www. infoplease.com/spot/northireland1.html

Chapter 7

1. Edwin Musoni and Ignatius, "Genocide Remains in Uganda Used for Witchraft Purposes," The New Times, 22 March 2009, URL: http://allafrica.com/stories/2009 03230005.html
2. Emmanuel Viret, Kayibanda, Grégoire, from The Online Encyclopedia of Mass Violence, published on 1 March 2010, URL: http://www.massviolence.org/Kayibanda-Gregoire
3. Lt. Gen. Romeo Dallaire with Major Brent Beardsley, *Shake Hands with the Devil: The Failure of Humanity in Rwanda* (Caroll & Graff Publishers, New York, 2004), 47-48.
4. Martin Meredith, *The Fate of Africa: A History of Fifty Years of Independence* (Public Affairs, New York, 2005), 487. For additional information on the history of the Rwandan genocide, see also: Immaculee Ilibagiza with Steve Irwin, *Left To Tell, Discovering God Amidst the Rwandan Holocaust* (Hay House Inc., Feb. 2006); Tracy Kidder, *Strength in What Remains: A Journey of Remembrance and Forgiveness* (Random House, 2009).

Chapter 8

1. Snakes, URL: http://en.wikipedia.org/wiki/Snake

Chapter 12

1. UNICEF, URL: http://www.unicef.org/search/search php?q=Rwanda&Go.x=0&Go.y=0 (accessed June 6, 2011).
2. Andrew Maykuth, *The Philadelphia Inquirer,* Sept. 6, 1998, "Rwanda: Aftermath of Genocide, Young Lives

Touched by Death, Part 1," URL: http://www.Maykuth
.com/Projects/rwan1.htm

3. Ibid.

4. American Psychiatric Association, *Diagnostic and Statistical Manual of Mental Disorders, DSM-IV-TR: The Current Manual*, Fourth Edition (American Psychiatric Association, Washington DC, 2000).

5. Charles Mugisha Buregeya, PR 646, Principles of Pedagogy, Summer 2001.

Chapter 14

1. *Tanzania/Uganda: Prevent Forced Return of Refugees,* Governments and UN Refugee Agency Should Urgently Clarify Refugees' Options Before Camps Close, June 19, 2009, from Human Rights Watch, URL: http://www. hrw.org/en/news/2009/06/19/tanzaniauganda-prevent-forced-return-refugees

2. World Health Organization statistics for Rwanda, URL: http://www.who.int/gho/countries/rwa/en/

Study Guide

by Susan W. Lester

How to Use This Study Guide

To make the most of this study guide, use it in a small group meeting once a week. This is a great way for you to be involved in The Great Commission since you will be discipling one another in the Word of God.

Commit to complete your assignments, listen to one another carefully, love and support one another, and pray for one another. You can't do all of these things perfectly, but without targets, we never hit the mark. Be careful not to share sensitive or personal information from group members with those outside, but we do hope you will recommend this study to others!

At the beginning of each week is a meditation passage. Find a way to look at it and think about it every day. Say it out loud, put it on a postcard and stick it to your mirror, write it on a piece of paper and put it in your jacket pocket or purse, type it on your Facebook screen, blog about it, or leave your Bible open to it on your office desk or kitchen counter. Then, whenever you notice it, read it. At lunch or at dinner, pray about it. Say it aloud in your car. Really take some time and think about what God wants you to learn. Talk to God about it at every turn.

Sprinkled throughout this study guide are Application Opportunities. We hope you will endeavor to follow through with these, putting hands and feet to your knowledge.

As Charles says, "Your Bible study isn't done until you go out and do it!"

For the next six weeks, we hope you will take time to read this book together and ponder these questions by yourself and with the Lord—praying for His guidance and revelation. Then share what happens with others in your small group.

As you take this journey with Charles Mugisha Buregeya—from the jungles of Uganda to the European continent, to the United States, and finally to Rwanda—may you be blessed, actively growing in the knowledge and faith of our Lord and Savior, Jesus Christ, God's one and only Son.

Week 1

Meditate on Matthew 28:18-20

And Jesus came up and spoke to them, saying, "All authority has been given to Me in heaven and on earth. Go therefore and make disciples of all the nations, baptizing them in the name of the Father and the Son and the Holy Spirit, teaching them to observe all that I commanded you, and Lo, I am with you always, even to the end of the age."

Day 1: Read the Introduction and discuss the following:

1. What is the "coffee" philosophy of Africa New Life Ministries International?

2. In February 2005, Dr. Jerry Rankin, President of the International Board of Missions, part of the Southern Baptist Convention, America's largest evangelical denomination with approximately 40,000 churches and nearly 16 million members, spoke on the Great Commission (Matthew 28:18-20) and told a group of pastors and church leaders: *"All the nations* really means all the people groups and all the cultural groups in all of the nations. The world is a waffle, not a pancake, so the Gospel must be carefully poured out across a nation to bridge all of the different cultural barriers and cultural differences." How does the ministry philosophy of Africa New Life intend to bridge these gaps?

Day 2: Reread the story of the ant and the elephant in the Introduction.

3. As you think about this story, ask God to reveal your status:
    A. I haven't climbed onto the elephant yet.
    B. I'm on the elephant, but I still act like I'm the one making a difference.
    C. I'm learning to give God all the praise and glory for my ministry opportunities and results.

4. Do I believe what I am doing is important to God? Why?

5. It took effort, step by step, for the ant to climb up on the elephant's back. As you consider this, what will help your faith increase? What steps should you take next?

Days 3-4: Read Chapter 1 and discuss the following:

6. A. As a young boy, what challenges did Charles face?
    B. What challenges did you face in your childhood?

7. How did Aloyizi protect his family? If your family was in danger because they attend a Christ-believing church, what would you do to protect your family members?

8. Does God protect a man before he even knows Him, let alone before he becomes a Christian? What verses from the Bible can you use to support your answer?

Days 5-7: Read Chapter 2 and discuss the following:

9. What betrayals did the family experience?

10. Have you ever been betrayed? What happened?

11. In Africa word travels fast from family member to family member. Why did the soldiers take the men and the cows away from the village and leave the rest of the prisoners unguarded?

12. How were the different Buregeya family members saved during the raid?

13. Read the story of the Good Samaritan in Luke 10:30-37. Who in this chapter most closely resembles the Good Samaritan? Why?

Application Opportunity

Is there someone you know who needs your compassion right now? What could you do for them? What will you do for them?

Week 2

Meditate on John 14:21, 23

He who has My commandments and keeps them, he it is who loves Me, and he who loves Me shall be loved by My Father, and I will love him and will disclose Myself to him… If anyone loves Me, he will keep My word; and My Father will love him, and We will come to him, and make Our abode with him.

Days 1-3: Read Chapter 3 and discuss the following:

1. Why did Charles struggle with Catholic training?

2. Read the following verses and list the letter for the corresponding truths (listed on p. 141) next to them.

Verses	Letter(s) from Corresponding Truth(s)?
Romans 3:23	
1 John 1: 5-10	
Romans 5:8	
Romans 6:23	
John 3:16-18	
John 14:21-23	

<u>Corresponding Truths</u>

A. If I love Jesus and obey Him, He will disclose Himself to me. I will know Him personally.
B. If I say I don't sin it means I don't know Jesus Christ personally because He is truth. So, the more I know Him the more I will see the sin in my life by contrast.
C. If I confess my sins to God, He will forgive me.
D. If everyone falls short of God's character and sins, then so do I.
E. God loves me even though I sin. He demonstrated that through the death of His Son Jesus Christ.
F. The price of sin is death, but God took care of this by giving me a free gift of eternal life in Christ Jesus when I make him my Lord.
G. God sent Jesus into the world to give me eternal life, not to judge me.
H. If I believe in Jesus Christ as the Son of God, coming from the Father, then I will not be judged by God; it is my belief or unbelief that will judge me before God.

3. Have you developed a true personal relationship with Jesus Christ directly confessing your sins to Him? Why or why not?

4. When Charles began to come to church, at first what kept him coming back?

Application Opportunity

Do you and your family help those who are new to feel welcome at your church? How can you sharpen your service in this area?

5. How did Mama Bunkenya get Charles to come to church?

6. Do you believe Satan hinders unbelievers from coming to church? What can you do about this?

Application Opportunity

Will you be willing to do what Mama Bunkenya did? If so, list four people you know who you can begin praying for, believing God will give you good opportunities to invite them to church.

A.

B.

C.

D.

Days 4-7: Read Chapter 4 and discuss the following:

1. As you read about Charles and his reluctance to share his testimony with his village, could you relate? What was it like for you the first time you told someone you were a Christian?

2. Read the following verses: *Therefore, since we have such a hope, we are very bold. We are not like Moses, who would put a veil over his face to keep the Israelites from gazing at it while the radiance was fading away. But their minds were made dull, for to this day the same veil remains when the old covenant is read. It has not been removed, because only in Christ is it taken away. Even to this day when Moses is read, a veil covers their hearts. But whenever anyone turns to the Lord, the veil is taken away. Now the Lord is the Spirit, and where the Spirit of the Lord is, there is freedom. And we, who with unveiled faces all reflect the Lord's glory, are being transformed into his likeness with ever-increasing glory, which comes from the Lord, who is the Spirit* (2 Corinthians 3:12-18 NIV).

This verse shows us that the life of a Christian should not be a stagnant one. As we read and study God's Word we will change. When you became a Christian did you change? How? If you have been a Christian for a long time, can you think of a recent change you have made (or are working on) because of God's guidance?

3. Charles was kicked out of his home because of the change his faith made in him. This was exceedingly difficult for an African first-born male and he refers to this as a time of persecution. How have you experienced rejection or persecution for your faith?

Application Opportunity

Will you be willing to do what Charles did and share your faith? List four people you know for whom you can pray, believing God will give you opportunities to share about Jesus Christ with them.

A.

B.

C.

D.

Week 3

Meditate on Matthew 17:19-21 and Hebrews 11:6

Then the disciples came to Jesus privately and said, "Why could we not cast it out?" And He said to them, "Because of the littleness of our faith; for truly I say to you, if you have the faith as a mustard seed, you shall say to this mountain, 'Move from here to there,' and it shall move; and nothing shall be impossible to you. But this kind does not go out except by prayer and fasting."

Without faith it is impossible to please God, because anyone who comes to him must believe that He exists and that He rewards those who earnestly seek him.

Days 1-3: Read Chapter 5 and discuss the following:

1. As you read this chapter, what did you learn about witchcraft?

2. Read Deuteronomy 18:9-12. Why were the people warned not to practice any of these things? According to Charles, who suffers most from witchcraft? Why?

3. What did the church do to "break the power of the evil one" in Gaba?

4. Read Matthew 17:14-21. What did the apostles have to learn to do before they would succeed in healing those who were demon possessed?

5. Consider these Scripture verses, and the three points that follow below: *Finally, be strong in the Lord, and in the strength of His might. Put on the full armor of God, that you may be able to stand firm against the schemes of the devil. For our struggle is not against flesh and blood but against the rulers, against the powers, against the world forces of this darkness, against the spiritual forces of wickedness in the heavenly places. Therefore, take up the full armor of God that you may be able to resist in the evil day, and having done everything, to stand firm (Ephesians 6:10-13).*

   A. What did Charles remember that helped him remain strong after the beating? What did he say to his fellow sufferers?
   B. Take time to think of the times God has provided, enabled, equipped, encouraged or helped you.
   C. For further study, read the entire passage of Ephesians 6. Ask God to show you how to put on your armor!

Application Opportunity

List the names of people you know who are struggling with an addiction. Then review the list from last week of the people you know who are without hope in Jesus Christ. Will you commit to fast and pray for them? If you have never fasted, could you take your lunch time and offer it to the Lord in their behalf instead of satisfying your own needs? Spend time praying for them by name and ask God to show you an act of compassion you can do for them or an opportunity to share John 3:16 with them and ask, "When will you receive Jesus Christ?"

Days 4-6: Read Chapter 6 and discuss the following:

1. How did Charles come to the decision to go to England?

2. What does Charles say about God and our prayers?

3. What were some of the similarities between The Troubles in Ireland and the genocide in Rwanda?

4. It took a lot of people to get Charles to England and Ireland. How is this related to his success in accomplishing what God has called him to do?

Day 7: Spend time in prayer today and discuss the following:

1. Does God want me to have a God-sized dream or to support someone who has one?

2. How can I help this generation know more about Jesus?

3. Do I have skills or talents that I am keeping to myself instead of using them for God's purposes?

4. Is something keeping me from doing what God is calling me to do?

5. Am I a sleeping giant? If so, why?

Week 4

Meditate on Psalm 10:17-18

O Lord you will hear the desire of the meek; you will strengthen their hearts, You will incline Your ear to do justice for the orphan and the oppressed, so that those from earth may strike terror no more.

Days 1-2: Read Chapter 7 and discuss the following:

1. What were some of the factors that contributed to the genocide in Rwanda?

2. The Rwandan genocide was particularly brutal. Many men, women, and children were murdered by their neighbors. Injustice is something that God abhors. In your Bible, find and list several passages about God's heart toward the innocent and those who commit injustices.
    A.
    B.
    C.
    D.

3. Why did Charles travel to Rwanda the first time? The second time? What did he decide to do after his second visit?

Application Opportunity

Take time this week to pray specifically for the victims of the Rwandan genocide. Ask God to protect them from evil, to bring them into deeper relationships with Jesus Christ, and to heal their nation. Ask God for an outpouring of His Spirit among the people.

Days 3-4: Read Chapter 8 and discuss the following:

1. How did Florence learn about becoming a Christian?

2. What situations deepened her faith in God?

3. Read how James, who lived with Jesus and knew Him all of his life, instructed the early church in James 1:22-25. Then read what Jesus said after the Last Supper in John 15:5-7. What is the connection between "doing" and "blessing"?

Application Opportunity

What should you be doing for Jesus? Spend time this week looking into your churches needs. Do you like children? Teens? Adults? Find out what needs to be done to help them learn about Jesus Christ. Or perhaps you could serve food, take care of the babies, put out the bulletins or pens in the pews, usher, greet people at the door and help them find their way. You can find many opportunities to "Do the Word of God!" Don't wait to be asked; Florence didn't. Volunteer! Your ministers will rejoice that one more saint has rolled up his or her sleeves!

Days 5-7: Read Chapter 9 and discuss the following:

1. Has God answered an important prayer for you as He did for Florence? Write down that experience and spend time thanking God for it.

2. Florence was redirected in her thinking by the woman she met in England. How?

3. If God asked, would you lay down your ministry or your favorite church activity right now? If not, who owns and is in charge of your ministry?

4. A miracle is *an extraordinary event manifesting divine intervention in human affairs*. Jesus performed many miracles to prove His Deity. Does God still perform miracles today? In what ways?

5. Is answered prayer a miracle? Always? Or only sometimes?

Week 5

Meditate on Proverbs 3:5-6

Trust in the Lord with all your heart, and do not lean on your own understanding. In all your ways acknowledge Him, and He will make your paths straight.

Days 1-2: Read Chapter 10 and discuss the following:

1. Why did Charles decide to go to seminary in Portland, Oregon?

2. Read Proverbs 3:5-6. How does this verse apply to what happened to Charles? Have you ever had a direction from the Lord that didn't make sense at the time? What happened?

3. How did Florence help Charles finish his challenge and go to Portland?

Application Opportunity

Take time this week to pray and ask God to show you anything you have allowed to prevent you from doing His will, from obeying Him, and from trusting Him. Besides confessing this as sin, what steps do you need to take to obey God now?

Days 3-5: Read Chapter 11 and discuss the following:

1. How did Africa New Life Ministries get its start?

2. What did Fred discover when he went to "Spy Out the Land?" Can you recall a time when God seemed to answer your prayer with a specific set of circumstances?

3. Why did Papa Bill get involved with Africa New Life Ministries?

4. When Papa Bill became involved in the first large project, what did he learn?

Application Opportunity

Is there something God has shown you that you have yet to act upon? Ask God for a new opportunity to follow through!

Days 6-7: Read Chapter 12 and discuss the following:

1. List some of the problems children in Rwanda face.

2. Read Matthew 9:11-13. According to Charles, how does this passage tie into picking coffee?

3. What is Africa New Life doing for the women and children of Kigali and Kayonza?

Week 6

Meditate on Matthew 11:22-24

And Jesus answered saying to them, "Have faith in God. Truly I say to you, whoever says to this mountain, 'Be taken up and cast into the sea,' and does not doubt in his heart, but believes that what he says is going to happen, it shall be granted him. Therefore I say to you, all things for which you pray and ask, believe that you have received them, and they shall be granted you."

Days 1-3: Read Chapter 13 and discuss the following:

1. Establishing the first ANLM church, which became The Dream Center, was a difficult process. What verses kept Charles going during the ups and downs?

2. What looked like the end of a dream ended up being a blessing. Has that ever happened to you? If so, how?

3. At the end of this chapter is a list of people from a variety of humble beginnings who achieved notable things. Why do

you think they were able to succeed? Do you think everyone around them thought they would succeed?

4. Look up a few of the biblical names in the list and check their stories from the Bible. What obstacles did they face?

Application Opportunity

Are there obstacles in your way right now? Do you want to live out your Christian faith? Begin today by praising God for the obstacles and asking Him to continue to guide you through them! Ask Him to remove them, use them, or help you carry them with you.

Days 4-5: Read Chapter 14 and discuss the following:

5. Read Isaiah 58:6-8 again at the beginning of this chapter. How is that passage related to what Africa New Life Ministries is doing in Kageyo?

6. How can you apply these same verses in your city or community? Does your church have a ministry among the poor? How can you help to strengthen that ministry?

7. One testimony is included of a mother who accepted Jesus Christ because of the ministry of Africa New Life in the Kageyo community. What else should be done to ensure she will continue to follow Christ and grow in her faith?

Days 6-7: Read Chapter 15 and discuss the following:

8. Take some time and try to out-imagine God, and then imagine a little more, and then imagine some more, stretching your imagination! God then says to you, "I can still beat you!" How does that affect your thinking?

9. In the sermon, which of the five people are you? Which one would you like to be? Which one do you think God wants you to be?

10. Charles talks a lot about dreams. Watch the video at africanewlife.org and see what this means to the children of Rwanda. What dream(s) can you make come true?

Application Opportunity

There are many opportunities for you to get involved with Africa New Life Ministries. Here are a few of the many opportunities listed on the africanewlife.org website.

A. You can sponsor a child and form an incredible lifeline to a family in Rwanda.
B. You can join a mission team and share the Gospel through worship.
C. You can deliver food to Kageyo.
D. You can hold the hands of street kids during worship.
E. You can sponsor or lead a medical team to minister among the poor in Rwanda.
F. You can commit to raise funds for any of a number of projects listed on the website.
G. You can invite your small group, Sunday School class, or church to make a difference!

Final Challenge

Rwanda needs God-sized miracles and the active support of God-believers to become a healthy, free, independent and God-fearing nation. Their children need to have dreams for tomorrow. Today, what can you do to help?

Let's Connect!

Again, thank you so much for reading this book. Now, we would love to hear from you!

You can contact Charles and Florence, learn more about one of ANLM's women's ministries, and inquire about sponsoring a needy Rwandan child. It takes just a few minutes.

Here's how…

Our mailing address:
Africa New Life Ministries International
7145 SW Varns St., Suite 201
Portland, OR 97223

Our website:
africanewlife.org

Our e-mail address:
book@africanewlife.org

Our phone number:
(503) 906-1590

After contacting us, please don't put this book away! Instead, please encourage a loved one or friend to read it, too. And please include Charles and Florence, and Africa New Life, in your ongoing prayers. Thanks!

9748532R0009

Made in the USA
Charleston, SC
10 October 2011